WINTER DAYS

IN

INDIA AND ELSEWHERE

WINTER DAYS

IN

INDIA AND ELSEWHERE

WILLIAM GEORGE BLACK

GYAN

Published by

Gyan Publishing House
5, Ansari Road
Daryaganj, New Delhi-110002
Phone: 011-47034999, 9811692060
E-mail: books@gyanbooks.com

Distribution Network
gyanbooks.com
India, USA, Canada, UK, Australia

ISBN: 978-93-7097-343-5 (PB)

First Published, 1908

2nd Impression 2025

Printed at: Gyan Press, Delhi.

WINTER DAYS IN INDIA AND ELSEWHERE
Arthur WILLIAM GEORGE BLACK

WINTER DAYS

IN

INDIA AND ELSEWHERE

BY

WILLIAM GEORGE BLACK

Privately Printed

GLASGOW
JAMES MACLEHOSE AND SONS
PUBLISHERS TO THE UNIVERSITY
1908

TO

A. R. B. B.

NOTE

Chapters I. to III. and V. to XI. appeared as Letters to the *Glasgow Herald*, and I have to thank the Editor for permission to reprint them. Chapter IV. is a summary from the Journal-Letters we sent home. Chapter XII. on Missions in India was written after my return and has not hitherto been printed in its present form. It formed the basis of addresses delivered to the Aberdeen Elders' Association on 21st October, 1907, and the Glasgow Elders' Association on 17th February, 1908.

W. G. B.

Ramoyle, Dowanhill Gardens,
Glasgow, *May*, 1908.

CONTENTS

APPENDICES

CHAPTER I

WINTER DAYS IN INDIA

Mount Abu, Rajputana, Dec. 5, 1906.

UNDOUBTEDLY if dirigible balloons become possible the ideal plan of travel for the luxurious tourist would be that his air-vessel should meet him somewhere in the Arabian Sea, and that from the deck of his P. and O. he should be whirled to this delightful mountain. He would avoid the very marked inconveniences of landing at Bombay, and the sweltering heat of that beautiful but trying city. Bombay lies like an Indian Venice in and on the sea, but the temperature is oppressively hot and moist to the stranger, whose slightest exertion is attended by profuse perspiration. The conditions are mitigated by punkahs and electric fans, with the result that you are in an incessant draught, and "stranger's cold" is (though in a different sense) quite as common as old travellers said it was in St. Kilda. In St. Kilda the natives suffered from the arrival of a vessel; in Bombay the visitors suffer from their own arrival. At this time of day one does not describe Bombay; its public buildings are magnificent, and the native city is a blaze of colour and a hive of industry. The privilege of membership of the Royal Bombay Yacht Club, with its beautiful turf and its admirable arrangements, must make all one's recollections of Bombay pleasant —barring the heat.

From Bombay we took the night train to Manmar, where we changed into the Nizam of Hyderabad's railway, and ultimately at a distance of 210 miles or so from Bombay reached Daulatabad. Above it, 500 feet high, rises a huge conical granite rock, and on it, and in it is a thirteenth century fortress. You enter by great doors, spike-protruding to resist elephants, then through gate after gate, each ingeniously hidden and guarded, you mount and pass the dwelling where the last King of Golconda was imprisoned for thirteen years. Then you cross an abyss—by a light stone bridge—which used in old days to be spanned only by planks, and enter the impregnable citadel itself, and through torch-lit tortuous rock passages go always upwards until a small plateau is reached. At last (and very tired) you attain a pillared court or pavilion, from which a glorious view is obtained over the flat surrounding country and the tiger-haunted slopes of the neighbouring jungle. This pavilion was the favourite residence of the Emperor Shah Jehan and his son Aurangzeb. The Nizam is said to the present day occasionally to administer justice on the summit of those wild precipices. From Daulatabad to Roza is only eight miles, but in the rough-hooded native dogcart or tonga, with all your luggage (including your bedding) slung round it, progress is very slow. The road is steep. Night had fallen, and the moon was shining brightly ere we entered the weird gate of the walled town of Roza, where in a topmost chamber of the gate some unseen singers were pouring out indescribable music to the scented air. We drove through the town to the Rest House, and the following morning visited the rock-hewn Temples of Ellora, twelve Buddhist, fifteen Brahmin, and five Jain, works hewn from the living rock. While all are wonderful, that of Kailasa is the most stupendous. It stands in a sort of pit, the back wall of which is a precipice 100 feet high. The Temple is 276 feet long and 154 feet broad, and all this is excavation and carving, not building. Here are huge stone elephants and monsters and the thousand-and-one gods and god-symbols in which the Hindu mythology revels. Up and down the temples scampers with lightning swiftness the graceful Indian squirrel, otherwise—but for some Brahmin who appears for gifts out of the darkness of the chambers surrounding the shrines—there is no life at all in this wilderness of imagery, which dates from the seventh and eighth centuries. For a mile and a half along the hillside there is temple after temple of the three faiths, none of which, be it observed, is in any way a dead faith at present; they have millions of devotees. From Ellora we stopped but a few minutes at Roza to visit the simple tomb of Aurangzeb, and then drove back to Daulatabad, and took train to Manmar, where we spent an exceedingly uncomfortable night in the waiting-room till 3.30 a.m., and then returned to Bombay. The excursion is one of the highest interest, but it is not easily made owing to the trains, the bad horses, and the extreme noise of the stations at night, where each train stops half an hour, and the native travellers, looking like the Forty Thieves in a pantomime, in all the wildness of Indian night attire (which is as voluminous by night as it is scanty by day) sit and talk at the pitch of their voices, assisted by all their relations and friends. The scene is one to dream of, but it effectually prevents dreaming.

From Bombay we started afresh for Ahmedabad;

again by night. On arriving we had baths and breakfasted at the station, and set out in a victoria drawn by capable horses along the dusty roads of a typical Eastern city. The sky was spotlessly blue this December morning, and the air sweet and not too hot. We passed camels waiting for their loads of merchandise; great monkeys came leaping from tree to tree to get the monkey-bread; green parrots perched on every doorway of each white temple; picturesque and slender pillars support little chambers like dovecots, elaborately carved, and form the Jain feeding-places for birds, which are among the peculiar features of this town of 186,000 inhabitants, with an area of two square miles on the left bank of the Sabarmati river. Travellers are grateful for guide-books, but they always quarrel with them. Murray says it is impossible to see Ellora in less than two days, while less will easily suffice so far as the caves themselves are concerned. On the other hand, to give only four hours to Ahmedabad is little short of madness. To come so far and not see this fairy city properly would be a strange injustice to one's self. It is above all the abode of cunning craftsmen in stone and wood and metals, and everything is beautiful and elaborate. Nor is the art a dead art. The Hathi Singh Temple was only finished in 1848 at a cost of a million rupees. It is a Jain temple exquisite in all its parts, full of variety and infinite in its expression of the artist's desire to do honour to the house of his God. To describe in what Jain worship differs from other Hindu worship would be here out of place. To go from the modern to the old, there is the tomb of Shah Alam, two miles south-east of the town; this Mahomedan saint died in 1495. The tomb is covered (like many others) by a cloth, which when lifted discloses the exquisite carving, fresh as when executed; the floor is black and white marble, the doors are of open brasswork, and the pure white marble walls are pierced and carved in an interminable series of varying geometric patterns, so that if ever marble looked like lace it is here; at Sidi Said's mosque, in the city, likewise the windows are filled with delicate stone tracery of tree stems and branches. To enumerate building after building would be a vain task. It is the unity of determination in the members of the three faiths to make beautiful places for their worship that is the striking feature, and the great success with which, under this cloudless sky, the artificers have been able to evolve indescribable combinations of dignity, grace, dazzling whiteness, is a refreshment to each religious sense to which they appeal. Here too, as in Bombay, is an Asylum for Animals, which contains sheds for about 800 animals. There is a room, says Murray, where insects are fed; but we did not penetrate there. We visited the Irish Presbyterian Mission Church, which has a native Christian village of 400 persons, and conversed with the headman of that village. We slept at the railway station at Ahmedabad, and, perhaps we are getting accustomed to Oriental crowds, for the noise disturbed us not in the least, and the next day we started for Abu Road Station, from which (sixteen miles) in two or three hours we drove to this place. There is only one small hotel, and that hotel is not in any way European, but Mount Abu is the headquarters of the Rajputana administration, and the hot-weather resort of many Rajahs, whose palaces crown the hills. The mountains occupy an area of about fifty miles in circumference, rising like an island out of the great, flat Indian plain.

Here we are 4500 feet above the sea, but the highest peak is over 5600 feet. The climate is absolutely perfect, fresh and invigorating, under a cloudless sky. A lovely lake, with little islands, lies in the heart of the so-called plateau, and is a lasting joy to the eye; and in the jungle, which covers all the hillsides, "bears, panthers, and tigers are to be found," as the railway guide-book concisely puts it. In this sequestered mountain are some of the most celebrated Jain temples in India, all of which we have visited. But this letter is already too long, and must end. Yes! to fly from the Arabian Sea direct to Mount Abu would be paradise indeed.

CHAPTER II

HIDDEN SHRINES AND SACRED WATERS

Udaipur, December, 1906.

In days of railroads we are apt to forget how distant and hidden were the Jain temples of Mount Abu. The railway only reaches Abu Road; after that you have a stiff climb to where, 4500 feet above the sea, and a couple of miles even from the small modern European summer resort, the temples of Dilwarra stand. Nineteen miles by tonga and 'rickshaw is a good distance for even the tourist; think of the remoteness of the temples to the dwellers hundreds of miles away from even the foot of the mountains, who were inspired with a desire to worship at Dilwarra in old days, before a railway came as it were tolerably near, and when the only road up the heights was a rough bridle-path! There are two temples, one built about 1032, and the other in the century following. The latter is a bewildering vision of slender white columns elaborately carved;

around the temple building is an oblong courtyard, with fifty-five cells, each containing a cross-legged image of Parswanatha. In the centre, at the end of a portico of forty-eight pillars, is the dark shrine. In front of the shrine on the day we were there were two bridegrooms giving thanks for their marriages. One was about six years old, and clothed only in a smile and a silver chain round his hips; he strolled about or played, his devotions being conducted by his mother. But the other bridegroom was about twenty-four years of age, and sat before a portable harmonium, which he had brought with him in a large Peek and Frean biscuit chest. He played vigorously with his right hand, and sang from his service book (which he held in his left) most stentoriously. Four women, seated at corners of his carpet, joined in. At intervals a priest near the entrance banged two big drums; other two rang bells, and a fourth clanged pieces of metal most sonorously. The noise was terrific. After he caught sight of us the melody of the excited musician seemed remotely to resemble "God Save the King," and perhaps the thank-offerer was of opinion that Parswanatha would not object to sympathetic loyalty being mixed with devotion. The following day we went, partly by 'rickshaw and partly on foot, to the still more remote temples of Achilghar, some seven miles from Dilwarra, before reaching which we visited Agri Kund, a tank famous in Hindu mythology. It is now ruined; the tank steps are broken, and the water is low and overgrown with green stuff, but on one side stand three large stone buffaloes, and near them is a marble relief of Pramar, with his bow bent. In the wild mountain jungle this ruined tank and the great stone beasts by its side are very impressive. Up steep open stairs we go to the temples. Those on the very summit, commanding a magnificent view, are Jain; those on the lower ground are (with one exception) Hindu. At the topmost temple we met the little naked husband of the day before still going the round of holy places with his pious mother. Not least remarkable here was a painting on an exterior wall of what might well have passed for a Hindu idea of the appearance of an Irish peasant, shillelagh, tall hat and all; and in the interior was the exact portrait of the King of Clubs. Over all was the glorious blue sky, and in the delightful air the little temple bells on standards on the roofs faintly jingled. We descended by a rough footpath to a cave in the mountain, where we found a fakir enjoying a pipe in a small cavern—his home for life. At his invitation I examined the numerous adjacent rough caves and holes where other fakirs live; for this hidden and distant place is of great sanctity, and the numerous devotees give the holy men many gifts. The caves were not unlike the caves in Mount Subasio, near Assisi, where St. Francis and his friends retired from time to time to meditate.

After a few delightful days at Mount Abu, we descended to the plains and travelled to Ajmere, with its little lake, on a high rock above which stands the Residency of the Governor of Rajputana. No rain fell in Ajmere for seven years until the last rains, and the lake dried up, but it is now full again, and very beautiful with the marble pavilions of the Emperor Shah Jehan by its side. While the mosque "of the two and a half days" (from the legend that it was built in that time) is notable for its glorious screen of seven arches, and the Dargah venerated alike by Mohammedans and Hindus is deeply interesting, nothing in Ajmere can move the visitor so much as a visit to the sacred lake of Pushkar, which lies seven miles from it. This is the most sacred lake in India, and must at one time have been well-nigh inaccessible except to very rich or patient pilgrims. Even now, though there is a well-constructed road, it is exceedingly steep and inches deep in fine dust. But what a way it is through the stern mountain pass with high gaunt rocks all around! You meet the strangest company; strings of camels; gaily-turbanned gentlemen on arabs; little native carts—like boxes—on which perhaps two women squat; lines of asses wood-laden; and you pass through a village where grey monkeys sit by the roadside and on the overhead branches. The variety is infinite. When the lake is reached you first pass through lines of sacred buildings and then—through a temple—emerge on broad steps which command the whole enchanting scene. There is the lake with lovely green islets before you; on all sides except your left is an infinite variety of temples built by different sovereigns in different centuries, all with broad terraced steps to the water. Up and down those steps stroll peacocks and cows; an occasional dog; a cat blinks from a ruin; the monkey-god grins at you with his foot on a jain-idol. You follow the Brahmins, who guide you around the lake (none but Brahmins live here); there are fakirs sitting in holes by the sacred water; there are vendors sitting in archways; everywhere is Oriental colour; there are ruins, but there is no filth, for the sun takes care of that. In one corner is a tank where half-a-dozen bronzed men are washing away their sins; in another is a covered place where queens bathe when they, like others, seek regeneration. On a green islet lie six or seven great alligators. Our Brahmin throwing crumbs into the lake showed us how the water literally boiled with fish, for, of course, no fish may here be caught. The splutter and bubbling reached the ears of an alligator, and he slipped gently into the water and made for us. As he came near the big jaws gave a snap, but—according to the Brahmin—the fish escaped (I was not so sure). There is no other place in India like this templed lake. I do not think there can be a more dreamlike place in the world as the sun sets and all its marbles are flushed with colour. If to mere English travellers the sheet of placid water appears so absorbing, what must it be to the pilgrims who, having heard of it from infancy, make their difficult way to it, through the wild mountains, at cost, inconvenience, and hazard,—for in the jungle there are all manner of wild beasts.

CHAPTER III

A NATIVE STATE

THE town and palaces of Udaipur, the capital of Mewar, stand on a beautiful lake. Within the town long strings of camels pass; sacred cattle take their quiet and honoured walk; great dogs fight with each other in clouds of dust; within the palace boundaries—as large as the city—you meet huge elephants very much at their ease, and green parrots are on nearly every roof; there are rows of stables of fine horses. Grey monkeys leap from branch to branch above the pillared tombs of the kings. On the distant side of the lake we saw last night just before sunset the wild pigs fed. Specially ferocious boars are kept in cells in the tower which overlooks the curious dust-enshrouded scene (such as Dante might have looked at in the Inferno); and in that tower is a hugh pit, with a guarded balcony above, from which one on occasion can survey the local royal sport of a tiger-and-boar fight. There is no lack of tigers on the hills close to Udaipur. The Maharana has a few cages of large leopards, tigers, and lions in the pretty public park. With such manifold varieties of animal life, the vivid and blazing colours worn by the people in turbans or robes, many of whom carry their long swords (as we bare umbrellas at home), from custom, or more correctly, as a hereditary Rajput right, make me despair of bringing home to you the kaleidoscopic brilliancy of life under the bright December sun, except by asking you to imagine a fancy dress carnival held by day in a zoological garden, with nearly all the animals loose! And above all the dust rises the height upon height of the sovereign's marble palaces, tier upon tier, colonnaded, shining, with the blue glittering lake beneath, dotted with green islets, each with a marble hall or summer quiet resting place, rich in orange trees now heavy with yellow fruit. In the town the great Jagannath temple is the centre of the worship of 46,000 people, and its pyramidal roof is seen from a great distance. Marble elephants flank the steep imposing stairs, which, as in all temples, make the approach. When you have not live elephants, or marble elephants here, you have elephants painted on each convenient space by the road—spirited, rushing elephants, each with a broken chain on one of his great hoofs; and in the entrance to the royal apartments is a gigantic image of Ganesh, the elephant-headed son of Siva, luck-bringing. But fine in its way as the Jagannath temple is the true charm of Udaipur lies in its palace courts. No lordlier pleasure-house than this could Coleridge have dreamt of, with its incomparable lakes, where the sun-descended monarch, who in his own person represents the premier house of India in point of blue blood, takes his ease. His Highness's architects and gardeners, it must be said, far exceed his house furnishers in taste, for it is little less than lamentable to find so many fairy chambers carpeted with no taste, and fitted with useless bric-a-brac, such as would sell at no English bazaar, each ticketed with its price "in plain figures." A crystal throne with red cushions provided for the use of the Prince of Wales finds its parallel in a crystal bedstead, surrounded by mirror walls, for the use of the sovereign's wife. But the eye finds relief in each chamber of unfortunate upholstery in the paradisaic view from the balcony of projecting window or terrace. Without all is lovely. There is another or upper lake, which in its wildness might be a Highland loch, except that Highland lochs have not marble summer-houses or a terraced marge.

From Udaipur we travelled to the old capital of the State, abandoned by its rulers over three centuries ago. There is no place where one can stay at Chitor itself, but at Chitorgarh, a mile or so away, there is a rest-house. A polite note to the Hakim was answered by the appearance of his very handsome elephant at 6.30 a.m.; but we did not start quite so early. Chitor lies on a rocky hill 500 feet above the surrounding country, and is approached through seven successive picturesque gateways; the table land of three and a half miles is now almost entirely either jungle or covered by ruins. The two great towers of Fame and Victory, the former eighty feet high, and dating from 890 A.D., and the other 122 feet high, and dating from 1440, are in admirable preservation. There is a temple to Kali, fresh stained with blood of sacrifice every morning yet, and ruins of a handsome palace with a curious zenana arrangement, which gave the ladies, who occupied chambers like loose-boxes, an opportunity of sitting in tiny balconies which look like eccentric external mangers. A long night journey brought us to Indore, the capital of Holkar's State, on Friday, 14th, in order that we might be present at the opening of the General Assembly of the Presbyterian Church in India, a union formed of all, or nearly all, the missions established or maintained by the Presbyterian Churches of Great Britain and Ireland and Canada. Regarding missions in India I make some observations in the last chapter.

CHAPTER IV

UP AND DOWN IN INDIA

WE left Indore on 17th December to return to the more usual tourist route, and for some hours the Canadian Missionary to the Bhils of Central India travelled with us. He is a real man. He was formerly a non-commissioned officer in the 18th Hussars; then a stationmaster in India; next a missionary. He and his wife and five children live far in the wilds. Some of his experiences would thrill a missionary meeting. His people believe in tree devils, and when the official among them who had a prescriptive right to make god-images and set them up, became converted, and set to work to cut down the sacred tree itself, the already converted flock sat round in a circle to catch the "bong" as it came out. They come to church each with his bow and arrows. They steal from each other in a systematic way; thus if B steals some of A's cattle, he in turns steals from C, and so on and on until A steals from off Z's cattle and everything is all square again. Christianity introduces a difficulty, for if one in the chain becomes a Christian, he cannot steal to replace what has been stolen from him, and this makes trials. One day our friend heard that a promising convert was raving drunk, and was swaggering about with a club declaring he would kill the missionary, a square set, sturdy, short man, who probably fears nothing in this world; he at once went to meet him. The Bhil swung his club and charged at him; the assailed stood his ground and knocked his assailant down. He rose and charged again. Again he was knocked down. Yet again he charged. The return blow was this time so convincing that the Bhil lay stunned. The victor dragged his foe by his heels to his wife and left him. The next day the sobered, battered Bhil came to beg forgiveness. "Certainly not," was the answer, "you tried three times to kill me yesterday, but I was stronger than you. You must show by your conduct that you are really sorry." That was three years ago, and since that time the Bhil never had transgressed in any way, and was in a sense a pillar of the church. At Christmas the teacher hoped to have a treat for his flock and had suggested a Christmas tree, but his wife said it must not be; they had taught the people that there were no tree-demons; if there was a Christmas tree, they would believe that after all the tree contained the Christian demon. A wise woman. So fearless are the Bhils that according to report they are nowadays never sentenced to death, for they regard death with indifference. The mission to the Bhils is not a widely known mission, but it is impossible not to believe in the good done by the admirable, energetic and sincerely pious ex-trooper.

On the 18th we reached Jaipur, the wonderful strawberry-cream-tinted city of Rajputana. A letter from Major Showers, the Resident, was handed me at the station, which stated that the Raj had put a carriage and pair at my disposal, with other courtesies, so after tiffin we left in state with two sais and a shield-bearer to visit Major Showers and Sir Swinton and Lady Jacob. The next day we visited the deserted city of Amber, and now a munshi or government clerk accompanied us and sat opposite us in the carriage, gleaming through enormous glasses. He was most polite and highly conscious of his honourable duties as guide, but his ideas and ours were not quite the same as to what we should see. He always wished us to "go to see gas-works!" but strange as it seemed to him, gas-works were the very last things we wanted to see. He told us many a singular story in a slow and carefully pronounced monotone, not the least curious being that of the Maharajah's elephants, which according to him are always ninety-nine in number. Sometimes an effort has been made to maintain an even hundred, but always the number reverts to ninety-nine; with such tales did our munshi—who informed me with pride he was "plucked B.A. Bombay University" —speed our way. Amber has been too often described for me to do so. The day was grey, but the place is wild and imposing.

In the afternoon we spent hours in the royal palace, which occupies one seventh of the whole city; never before have I been so completely transported to the middle ages, for in one corner men were repairing chain armour, in another scribes were copying MSS.; at the foot of the elaborate and rather tiresome gardens is a moat with huge alligators which were exhibited by an old attendant who is their very good friend; legend says it was to this moat that in pre-British days inconvenient palace personages were taken. Of the tombs of Jai Singh and the late Maharajah many have written, and the Observatory of the former lives in one's memory as no other observatory in the world can ever do.

From Jaipur we travelled to Agra, and after a visit to the great fort, where no native is permitted to enter without a pass—beautiful in palaces and mosques, and in its distant view of the Taj Mahal —we went to the Taj itself. It is the one building in the world that cannot disappoint. Photographs distort and cannot suggest the true rich colour, and pictures cannot give sufficient foreground without diminishing the apparent size of the principal building. As a matter of fact, the Taj seems to grow before the eye as you look, until you realise that despite the perfection of proportion (which misleads the eye) it is a very great building; white, shining and glorious, covered with exquisite work, inlaid, carved, and pierced marbles. It is to attempt the impossible, however, to describe the effect of perfection which the Taj produces, aided by the long, thin stream of water which reflects the front and the blue of the sky all around. It has always to be borne in mind that the Taj is not one building; it is part of an elaborate architectural scheme, with a great gateway a long way in front of it in red sandstone, and a mosque in red on one side and a hall like a mosque on the other, and behind, lower, is the broad river Jumna. All this grouping cannot, of course, be shown in any picture unless it were of enormous size. On the evening of Sunday we visited the Taj Mahal again, which we saw, quite alone, in moonlight, when it gleamed like whitest ivory. Of course we visited Fatehpur Sikri, a city 22½ miles from here, built by Akbar, and deserted by him twenty years after. This was our third deserted city. It is full of magnificent palaces, and according to local authorities is the abode of panthers, porcupines, serpents, etc. A young German on a month's holiday from Burma brought us back by motor car, and we greatly astonished a stately camel, whose expression of disgust at motor-speed was singularly fine.

On Christmas eve we reached Delhi; it was very cold, and I was glad to be warmly wrapt up in my fur coat. But on Christmas morning again all was delightful, with the brilliancy that only is found in the East. When in my bath I heard a distant military band playing "Bonnie Dundee," and home seemed not so very far away. Paulo presented each of us with a rosebud by way of Christmas greeting. St. James's Church was well filled, and prettily decorated with flowers. After service we went to the Fort, and visited the lovely buildings; they are of earlier date than those of Agra, but perhaps even more magnificent. The custodier is an old soldier, an Elgin man named Black, who left his native city in 1864. He has been out here forty-four years, and I should think would never return to Scotland. Here the terrible mutiny time is always with us. Behind us in church this morning was a memorial tablet to an entire family—husband, wife, mother-in-law, four sisters-in-law, four brothers, nephews, grandchildren, etc.—"brutally murdered on or about 11th May, 1857," and everywhere are similar records. What has been so often described need not here again be written of. All we could see, we saw. Our excellent friends, Mr. and Mrs. Cremer (he was formerly Dutch Minister for the Colonies), invited us to accompany them one evening to a private nautch. It was of a very sedate and demure description given by three girls and two sets of musicians. The entertainment consisted largely of movements of hands and fingers, and even of toes, but very little in the way of steps. There was also a good deal of discordant singing. The principal girl did a sort of snake-charming representation very cleverly. Perhaps the funniest thing was the promptness with which, at the close of the performance, the girls dropped off their finery and calmly stood up in a "shift" and meagre pants.

After a few days' stay at Delhi we arrived at Amritsar one Friday morning, and went to the Cambridge Hotel.

We had to wait an hour for our room, and nearly as long for breakfast; but ultimately we got comfortably settled, and then set off in a carriage for the Golden Temple, the centre of Sikh religion. All round a very large tank is a white marble platform, and at one place a broad white marble causeway leads to the temple, which is thus a sort of island in itself. It is all glittering without, and inside continual prayers are offered over the Holy Book of the Sikhs; of course our shoes had been removed before, and we went about in loose slippers. Garlands of roses and marigolds were thrown round our necks, and we were presented with white cups of sugar candy with candied sugar inside. We went up to a gallery and saw the very extraordinary groups below, all picturesque and earnest. In a corner of the gallery a holy man was perusing another enormous copy of the Book. We went a long way in slippered feet round the tank to a tower, richly embellished with Sikh pictures. At tiffin Mr. Casson, the Commissioner, called and offered to go with us again in the afternoon. So we went in great state and were received by all the chief priests; gold embroidered cloths were placed on the places where we sat, under the ugly red Victoria Memorial Tower, while our shoes were removed, and where we received one garland of flowers before we received two now, and presents of silk gauze scarfs. All the treasures were exhibited, the golden doors used on special occasions, the jewelled crown to be hung over the Book, the golden peacocks, golden staves and gilded punkahs, sacred swords, the treasury, etc. A most dream-like day in every way, outrageously and impossibly Oriental, and always the fakirs and beggars, the strange men from Ladak, the priests with extraordinary high hats like wizards in fairy tales, the still water, the glittering temple, and the venerable sages. Then we went to a shop and made some purchases, the seller squatting on the floor and his rivals standing at the door ready to burst upon us when we came out with narratives and warnings of the seller's well-known duplicity. He presented me with a receipted account, although, in fact, the price was not to be paid until we received the things in Calcutta. I pointed out this to him. He replied: "It is no matter; English gentleman!" Such is the credit of Englishmen shopping in India. In the evening we dined with the Commissioner. After stopping a few hours at Lahore, where Captain and Mrs. Elliot met us with a carriage, and we drove through the park and to some of the principal shops, we left again for Rawal Pindi, where Captain Charteris met us. After church the following day, Captain Charteris took us a most comprehensive drive round the very large military station, and in the evening we went to the Scotch service in the Army Prayer-room (see Chapter XII.). There was most beautiful moonlight both going and coming. We went to bed in our waiting-car at the station, where Paulo had our beds prepared. At about 6.30 a.m. the train started, and before lunch we arrived at Lahore, and found that our quarters at Government House were for that night to be in tents, but this was no hardship as we had two large tents, with bathrooms attached, the second tent being a combined sitting-room and bedroom. To the Governor's ball we were conveyed in bright moonlight in his celebrated camel carriage, drawn by four stately, soft-stepping camels, each with its driver in the Governor's livery. The ball was given in the Montgomery Hall—a fine building—and the guests numbered something like 700. I don't know when we have enjoyed a ball so much, but we left as soon after the Governor as we could, and were in our tent by 1 a.m. or soon after. The dancers kept it up till 4 or 5.

Next day we went to Nedan's Hotel to meet a friend from Peshawar, who lunched with us. A fortune-teller read our hands. A. is to have great luck about 20th January, including receiving "many many picture post-cards." She is to live to 105, but I go at 94. Six banks are to keep my money, and jewels also are to be mine in profusion. I have four friends, one of them a native. Now, who can that be? I am sometimes "mouth-angry" but never "heart-angry." I am very "happy with my lady," but "a lady at another station is very fond of me"—a rather embarrassing statement in A.'s presence. All bad luck is past for both of us. Then we went to the Fort and saw all the wonderful buildings it contains, including a curious armoury, chiefly of Sikh weapons, some of them very odd, such as a big pistol which was also a short sword; a crutch which was also a poinard, walking-stick swords, etc., etc. The great mosque, built by Aurungzeb, has a collection of Mahommedan relics—a hair of the Prophet's beard, Fatima's prayer mat, etc., etc. At Government House we had been transferred to a very spacious apartment about 30 feet high, and we had each a large bathroom and dressing-room. The centre of this house was once the huge chamber above a tomb. Then it was built round and added to and altered, and the result is that the dining-room and drawing-room are magnificent indeed. The former can dine 80 (that number dined there a week or two ago); it was decorated by Kipling's father, and the electric light is very ingeniously placed in the lofty domed ceiling.

We spent interested hours in the museum, Mr. Brown, the curator, showing us round. We saw what was to us quite a new section of Indian archaeology, namely, the examples from Peshawar, and elsewhere of Graeco-Hindu (Graeco-Bactrian) art, taking one back to the time and influence of Alexander the Great, and of the colonies he left after his brief victorious expedition. The "Fasting Buddha" is itself alone worth a journey to Lahore. Sir Charles Rivaz kindly gave us the use of the state elephant to visit the native bazaars. Lahore is one of the most Oriental of cities, and nothing could be more picturesque than those quaint, narrow, crowded streets. Often there was little more than room for us to pass, and repeatedly our driver hacked down strings of advertisements which obstructed our passage. From Lahore we followed the usual course in visiting Lucknow and Cawnpore. In each, the scenes of so much horror are now delightful gardens. Of Benares everybody writes. It is at once the most fascinating and the most repulsive place in India. The so-called monkey temple teems with unrestrained monkeys, which make one glad to leave the horrid precincts. Nor is the temple of the sacred cow much more pleasing.

We dined at the Central Hindu College. The party consisted of Mr. Arundale, his aunt, and Miss Herrington, "all cranks" they described themselves to be; but the fact is they are all Theosophists, and give their lives to teaching in their College without fee or reward. Mrs. Besant was at Madras. The next morning after breakfast we drove out again to visit the School and College. The object is to teach *pure* Hinduism. It is not a Christian College. It is a college to teach through English the "pure" principles of the Hindu religion and is a curious and interesting experiment which seems to be successful. The Prince and Princess of Wales visited the place last year, and the King has sent it an excellent portrait with his autograph. All the distinctions of caste are carefully observed. The bed-rooms of the boys (who get up at 4.30 and 5 a.m., but do not wash till 8) are extremely simple, but very tidy and very loyal with royal portraits. No corporal punishment of any kind is inflicted. There is a good laboratory; the boys play cricket, football, and hockey. They have a little temple in which the goddess of Wisdom is to be put, but it is not yet consecrated. They have, however, their priest, and a room for the boys' devotions. We heard some of the boys read, and saw them modelling, etc. A. alone was permitted to enter the girls' school, which is as secretive as a nunnery. There were about ninety little Hindu girls who answered demurely to stately names, and some six older girls, but the difficulty is to get girls to stay on, as the desire is to marry them off at once. The school has a printing press of its own; the boys look bright and happy. After all the purpose of the institution is much like that to which many Christian missionaries devote themselves, viz., secular education; but the Theosophists seek to make no converts, but only to make Hindus *good* Hindus. We spent a morning on the Ganges, and floated down its broad bosom about half-past seven a.m., past the ghats which line one side of the stream, each with broad steps to the water; above is a mass of temples and palaces, built by princes of such states as Indore, Jaipur, etc., for their people to stay in when they come to bathe in the sacred river. The great buildings, some crumbling, some in good order, extend for about a mile and a half, and the shores were thronged with people bathing and washing, and always praying, in or out of the water. Many fakirs were there. I saw the celebrated one who lies on a bed of big nails.

He is a stalwart fellow and was milking a sacred cow, for milk is the only food he takes; by-and-bye he strolled back to his painful couch and sat down lightly enough, and unwound his tremendous hair, never cut since he was born; coiled round his head, the hair must make a pillow proof against even big nails. Princes come to pray beside him and give him gifts, and he blesses them. He was virtually quite naked except for a small loin cloth. Another fakir spent his time bending backwards and forwards in a style any exponent of morning health exercises would much admire. The scene in the cold morning light was wonderful. At the burning ghat we saw two corpses consumed. The relations sat on the roof of a small temple like crows and watched silently and reverently the pyres. Sometimes a party of six was passed, in single file led by a priest (wearing of course no priestly robes of any kind); they were on their way to visit all the sacred places on the Ganges; one such procession consisted of four ladies with two stalwart men servants behind them, carrying all the party's bedding, for *that* is never left behind.

After a few days in Calcutta, where we dined with Sir Andrew Fraser, Lieutenant-Governor of Bengal, we went to Darjeeling, and were fortunate to have delightfully clear weather, so that Kinchinjanga, in all her majesty of snow and peak, 28,000 feet, was always visible. One night we had in the open an exhibition of weird Thibetan dances in the dark. The dances seem to be a survival of an ancestor of our Christmas pantomime, for they excelled in huge animals of basket-work presumably, with men inside, and in youths who simulated both horse and rider, and a peacock who ran cackling about, laying eggs (!). From Darjeeling we visited the Missions at Kalimpong and went on by the Teesta valley to Siliguri, whence we travelled to Dhubri-ghat on the Brahmaputra; we had a long, long wait on the sandy, sun-baked, mosquito-haunted flat there till about 3 p.m. we got on board the mail steamer; not until 4 did we leave, instead of at 9 a.m., as we had hoped. We were the only Europeans on board, even the captain being a native. We had excellent cabins, and felt as if we were on board a yacht, for this "Pegu" is only six months old; built by Denny of Dumbarton.

Our voyage lasted nearly two days on the Brahmaputra, a very great river, with for the most part low grey shores, on the sunniest of which lay many and many a big alligator. At first we could scarcely believe our eyes that the numerous log-like things were alligators at large, but we were quite close enough to see them stretch their legs and move rapidly into the water as we passed. Most of the land was arid waste, only varied by impenetrable jungle. The rest was delightful for us, after much land travel but we were disappointed to get to Gauhati—the prettiest reach—when it was dark, and we were pressed for time. The scenery round Gauhati is really fine, and there are some good temples could we have seen them. From Gauhati we took train to Titabur, through wildest jungle, and one recalls in particular the vision of a death-like pool in the forest where a motionless bird sat on a dead branch above the wan water.

At Titabur I visited my brother, who is a tea-planter, and as the house is a typical tea-planter's bungalow I may describe it. The wide verandah forms a large open-air drawing-room. The house stands high on posts, but the lower part is not entirely open space, for my bath-room was there and a bachelor's bed-room, and stores and other places. On the verandah level is the drawing-room to the right, with a regular tiled fire-place, in which a cheerful coal-fire was kept burning; to the left is A.'s little boudoir sewing-room, and beyond is the dining-room. Behind the dining-room is our host's very large bed-room, which was given up to us, with a bath-room for my wife on the same level, and my bath-room at the foot of an interior staircase. Opposite our room was our host's room. The verandah in front is very high, and the roof projects over the steps and far out so as to take carriages under its wide sweep. Around is cleared ground, with a level lawn-tennis ground duly laid out, and beyond is a vegetable garden. At the sides and back are numerous subsidiary buildings, such as the kitchen, etc. Two long-legged, broad-winged adjutant birds stood nearly all day on a roof, and there were two monkeys, each with a pole of his own, and a sort of box home on the top of the pole. Tea bushes meet the eye at a reasonable distance in front of the house, and beyond that is thick wooding, and yet further, as a matter of fact, is impenetrable virgin jungle, not the scrubby, shrubby jungle of Central India, but the real article of boys' story books, with wild elephants at large, and tigers and leopards "all proper." There are dusty roads, half mud with a day or two of welcome rain (no rain had fallen since October). There are many gardens like this in the neighbourhood, and there is a village and bazaar which is filled on Sundays by traders from all the country round.

The household was thoroughly well ordered, and we got better cooked food and much more appetising than in any hotel in India. The life seems an ideal one for a strong healthy man with all his wits about him and his gun always ready at his hand. As we were only three-quarters of a mile from the station, one never knew when a guest might arrive, for in Assam all passers-by must call. Assam is quite unlike any other part of India we visited, and the people are as different from the Thibetans as the Thibetans are unlike the Bengali, or the Bengali unlike the warlike Rajpoots or fierce Afghans. At Titabur we were some 70 miles from China.

Wild elephants are a serious nuisance in Assam, but we only saw one elephant here, and that belonged to the Forest officer. Tigers, jackals, and elephants and leopards are plentiful, and rhinoceros is shot lower down the Brahmaputra.

One day a conjuror performed in front of the verandah. As one of Robert's house servants afterwards said, "it was true magic." To learn such magic one goes to the country of Gora, where there are no men, only women; men who go there become sheep during the day, and at night they learn magic. They cannot get away, because if they start in the night they always find in the morning that they are where they were when they started. But if they go to a very, very old woman she may help them to escape, and then they become conjurors in India. However, our conjuror yesterday made no fairy-tale claims. He professed to come from Agra. He did the mango tree trick very cleverly indeed, and made a little duck of clay move about in a bowl of water to his command; extracted large iron balls from his mouth, apparently created three pigeons on the spot, and did many other wonderful things.

In the afternoon we went to the village school of which Robert is the over-authority, and the children turned out to do some sort of health exercises on the road. They were very funny, for they were adapted to Indian ways, and sometimes the children jumped along like frogs in a way no English child could do, or crawled and wriggled flat like alligators.

The people about here wear enormous hats, some are nearly five feet broad; they are very neatly made, and cost about three rupees.

The wild Nagas of the neighbouring hills are particularly fond of dogs for eating, and even pariah or "pi" dogs (which are not necessarily ownerless by any means) seem to know this, and give Nagas a wide berth.

On returning to Calcutta we were present at the State ball given by Lord Minto, where the Amir of Afghanistan was decidedly the principal figure.

After the State quadrille there was a pause, and the Afghan March announced the arrival of the Amir at his first ball! He looked as happy as a boy. His early trouble was whether to keep his round hat off or on. He looked better with it on, and evidently was advised that it was right to wear it. Everything and everyone appeared to offer him the utmost enjoyment. When we left about 1 a.m. he was still there, and seemed likely to stay. Of course the Mintos had to stay too. We enjoyed the ball thoroughly.

Next morning, 10th February, we left for Rangoon, on the "Taroba," being examined by a lady doctor before going on board in case we had plague.

CHAPTER V

BURMA

Rangoon, February, 1907.

"LITTLE they know of England who only England know," sings the poet with admirable truth. So, too, little they know of Glasgow who have not seen Burma. The headquarters of that great fleet which carries civilisation nine hundred miles up the Irrawaddy is in Glasgow; all its ships are Clyde built; the machinery in the mills of Rangoon bear Glasgow names; the million tiny candles which burn before the shrines in the great pagoda are said to be manufactured by the oil company which is as distinctively Glasgow-conceived as is the flotilla; every leading Rangoon merchant is the nephew or the cousin of some Glasgow citizen; it was a Glasgow youth who first greeted me on the lawn of the Gymkhana Club. Where Glasgow men go, Glasgow newspapers will follow; still, it was with something like surprise I recognised in Mandalay market a somewhat familiar type in a sheet underlying a pretty Burmese girl's wares; it was an ancient *Glasgow Herald*; and on one of the shrines of the Shwa Dagon itself I found a page of an antique pink *Evening Times* used as a cloth for offerings of Burmese charity. Burma, as every child knows, is a province of the Indian Empire, but much as India differs in herself, widely dissimilar as are, for example, Rawal Pindi and Benares, or Rajputana and Assam, yet Burma is un-Indian rather than India varied. You go to Burma by sea, as you go to Great Britain. When you arrive you are enveloped in a sweltering, moist, hot-house air, which is unlike the exhilarating Indian winter; the people are plump and good-looking and merry, their religion finds expression in the erection of countless quite un-Indian pagodas; they go clad in pink silks; the priests are in yellow (and every Burman at some period or other of his life is expected to be a priest). There is geniality and indolence everywhere, and luxuriant Nature says, "You do well to enjoy me." The trader scoffs and says, "The Burman is a lazy beggar; he will not work; to get men for our business we have to draw too liberally upon Madras and Chittagong." But why should the Burman work for others when his own very simple wants are so easily satisfied. Satisfaction! that is the keynote of Burma. "Be content with your lot," say our preachers at home. "I am content," says the Burman, "quite content." The European illogically answers, "But you should not be content." Who is to pronounce judgment upon those happy folk? Time was when Burmese armies poured into Assam and devastated that fertile country; but who wishes those days back? The Burman is no longer a soldier; he is a contented, happy citizen (with the exception afterwards to be noted); he abhors both milk and honey (as taught by his religion), and anyone who told him that a land of milk and honey was to be desired would fill him with horror; his fields yield richly to the minimum of toil; the rivers give him fish. He is healthy and strong and always a gentleman; his women have no caste or other restriction; they look after his affairs; keep his accounts—when he has any; smoke cigars enormously bigger than any men's, and withal are the perfection of neatness, and in their gay dresses flutter about like gorgeous butterflies. I can understand the aspirations of Rangoon merchants that Burma should be made a Crown Colony independent of India, but I am sure it would not affect a Burman one way or other.

We went to Mandalay by train; that city is desolated by plague, and the markets are half empty. A malicious bazaar rumour ran that a Royal personage who some time ago visited Burma saw so many Burmans he was afraid, and said the number must be reduced. Hence the plague. The fact is the plague is not the only trouble. The authorities, properly anxious to keep it within limits, sent emissaries far and wide to warn the people of danger and to teach them precautions. Unfortunately, those men were Indians, not Burmans, and the Burmans dislike Indians very much. So between plague and fear of plague and plague precautions, the markets of Mandalay are half deserted, and people have taken to the jungle. Hence want; hence a recrudescence of dacoitry; hence an organised attack to upset and rob the train by which it happened we were travelling. Fortunately the military police got wind of what was going on, and our train was boarded in the small hours of the morning by a strong force. The train was not upset, but we were hours late in reaching Mandalay. There have been several other attempts; fortunately all have been frustrated. But dacoitry is exceptional.

He who wishes to see Mandalay palaces must come quickly. In King Theebaw's time most of the city was within the picturesque walls. Troops cleared this great enclosure of all but the palaces and royal tombs, and our Government built great bazaars outside. Thus the city is entirely modern, with long, wide, straight, dusty, unromantic streets, along which runs an electric tram service. It is scarcely necessary to say that Kipling's flying fish might just as reasonably be looked for at Charing Cross as in Mandalay. Inside the walls (girdled by a moat on which grow the lotus lily) are the palaces of Theebaw—empty, looted, stripped. Here stood the throne from which the King through an opera glass (a disconcerting toy) surveyed Europeans approaching him on hands and knees; there were his audience chambers; here again is the graceful hall of his dancing girls; there is the dainty spire which Burmans know as "the Centre of the Universe." But, remember, it is all of teak —invaluable, magnificent teak, which makes the eyes of Rangoon teak merchants sparkle with desire and envy. Now the rich gilding has been stripped or has faded, the jewels and silks are in museums, and, despite the precautions which Lord Curzon, to his honour, instituted, some day or other this last shell of Burmese regal magnificence will be destroyed by fire. Mandalay will certainly flourish more and more each year as the commercial metropolis of Upper Burma, but when a conflagration next rages it will be no more a place of romance and palace secrets. The quaint magnificent Court dresses are already things of the past; the wife of the King's Commander-in-Chief keeps a curiosity shop; the daughter of one of his great nobles sells rubies in the verandah of the little hotel.

From Mandalay we went up the Irrawaddy—river of ages—by cargo steamer, which is rather three vessels than one, for on each side is a large float, each of which is a floating bazaar, the one of clothes and silks and hats and tools and all such things, and the other of vegetables and fruits and the like. Each night the steamer halts at an appointed bank; slim "water-boys" leap from the bows and carry ropes ashore and up the crumbling banks, on the top of which stand radiant groups of villagers in pink and white and blue, with a golden-robed, umbrella-covered, shaven priest or two, each with his attendant youth. Above shines the roof of a pagoda, on which a hundred little bells are tinkling, with its corners guarded by four huge monsters, all agape. At sundown the villagers come and go, making their purchases and listening to the Captain's gramaphone. Behind those occasional villages is nothing but wild jungle with wilder beasts; teak forests, where the trees whose wealth is to fall into Scotch pockets at home, are tended by isolated groups of capable young fellows —gentlemen bred, all of them—whose one certain place of meeting, sometime or other, unfortunately, is Mandalay Fever Hospital. There is but one good carriage road, and that is from the river bank up to the Ruby mines, and it is very good.

How magnificent is the scenery on this leisurely week's journey up the river! Infinite varieties of green in the luxuriant vegetation, and again and again amidst it the "flame of the forest," the splendid scarlet of the wild cotton tree. At night you see lurid spots on distant hills; those are forest fires, which gleam as if you were gazing on some burning mountain. At Bhamo the Irrawaddy passenger service ends, and one is within thirty-seven miles of the Chinese frontier. Here are Shans and all manner of curious folk, tiny-footed Chinese women, forest Burmese. Shall I tell of Burmese "football" played by five or six gay, slim, active youths with a cane ball, which they catch on their heads, their shins, their calfs, their necks, anywhere but on their feet? It is the universal game; I wished to buy one of the balls, as I might easily have done, but a youth promptly stopped his game and presented the ball as a gift, with the true

Burmese courtesy and grace. You laugh to a little naked boy sitting with his parents, and immediately he is made to stand up and return the Sahib's salutation with a proper salaam. It is impossible not to delight in those charming people. They may be idle, but it does one's heart good to see so much happiness. I do not forget the dacoits, but they are a small folk, an incident of the period of plague, and nothing more.

CHAPTER VI

SINGAPORE AND JOHORE

March, 1907.

I CANNOT but recall with shame that in writing from Rangoon I did not do more than mention the Shwa Dagon Pagoda nor its Golden sister at Mandalay. But who is to describe the indescribable, for each of those great temples is not one building—each is a courtyard approached by long flights of stairs, roofed with gilded and carved teak, guarded by monsters, and full of stalls of devout and secular dealers. In the centre of the courtyard rises the main pagoda, but around it is an infinite maze of other pagodas, small and great, and shrines of calm contemplative Buddhas. Here is a hall of rich statues, or, again, one sainted figure sits by himself. There are wood carvings of the most delicate tracery; there are grotesques which will haunt your dreams all your life long; there are aged pietists seated on the ground mumbling prayers and occasionally clashing a bell to call attention to the manner in which they are acquiring merit; there are dainty groups of Burmese ladies all a-flutter with cloud-like silks as they kneel or prostrate themselves at their devotions; there are naked children, cigar-sellers and toy-vendors, all the varieties of life of Burma. One goes again and again to the Shwa Dagon, but Kipling got no further than its steps in describing it, and one does not wonder.

The voyage from Rangoon to Singapore took some four or five days. We only stopped a couple of hours at Penang. At Singapore the brilliancy of the green grass at once surprises and delights the eye accustomed to the burnt-up soil of India. But it is explained by the fact that while Singapore seems almost intolerably hot to the visitor, yet it has a heavy tropical shower every day. Hence its greenness; hence, too, which is less delightful, its steaminess as of the moistest and hottest of hot-houses at home. The settlement is, of course, very modern. In a century a colony does not gather antiquity, but it is full of life and vigour. The season of depression from over-speculation in land has passed, and Singapore is now on the rising wave of rubber-growing prosperity. The Malay States, too, of which it is virtually the capital, are flourishing exceedingly. The health of the community is very good; the mosquitoes are intolerable, but they are not malarious; there is no plague or fever. I was speaking to a resident, formerly of Glasgow, who has lived in the island since 1873, and in all that time he has only, he says, been one week away from business from ill-health, and he has only once gone home. Certainly all the white population, ladies and men alike, look surprisingly fresh and vigorous, and this they attribute to the very thing which tries so severely their visitor, viz., the excessive humidity. There are great wide roads most beautifully smooth and well kept, handsome public buildings, and a general air of prosperity. The universal carriage is the rickshaw, drawn by young Chinamen with the finest and strongest legs in the world, one must think, and next to no brains. The Chinese are the universal servants, for the Malay, like the Burman, does not see why he should work for the white man when he does not require to do so for his own needs.

We went one night to the Malay theatre, where the "Merchant of Venice" was played in Malay. What Irving missed! What Beerbohm Tree has to learn! Among the incidental novelties, Shylock, Antonio, and Bassanio sang their parts to each other to modern waltz airs; but at intervals the action of the play stopped altogether, and two weird children came on to sing an American coon song; that finished amid loud applause, Shakespeare was resumed. Under such circumstances little wonder that the performances usually go on till two a.m. Portia was a little difficult to identify at first, but we found her at last in a plump and serious Malay girl with a wealth of heavy black hair hanging down her back and a very short skirt; she had however, magnificent gold anklets, and sat in a sahib's cane arm-chair with the dignity which befitted the lady of Belmont. She also sang several ballads in Malay, which I cannot think were Shakespearean; so, too, each suitor in the casket scene covered his sorrow by a judicious interjection of a pathetic or comic song, and Portia joined frankly and openly in the merriment. I cannot say of Shylock "this was the Jew that Shakespeare drew," but he was vigorous. The Malay scene-painter's Venice had been developed out of his inner consciousness of what Venice should be, and certainly St. Mark's Piazza might be improved by a large group of tropical plants in the centre. A "Street in Venice" owed something naturally to Singapore —particularly as regarded a large Union Jack on the top of a small hillock at the extremity of the perspective. But why cavil? It was a street, and would not any street in Venice or otherwise be improved by the Union Jack in full flow? I am glad I saw the "Merchant of Venice," but I am sorry I did not see "Hamlet," for there must be great capabilities in it, from a Malay point of view.

Singapore was originally leased as a marshy island from the Sultan of Johore, and his descendant is still an independent sovereign (with limitations). A short railway journey of less than an hour, stopping at jungle stations with such names as Cluny, Woodlands, etc., brings one to the narrow strait which separates Singapore from the mainland of Asia, and a ferry steamer takes the visitor quickly across. The Sultan kindly sent a very smart Malay A.D.C., in the smartest of khaki uniforms, to meet us with a carriage, and we saw everything in the State with great completeness, except the crown, which stands in a safe of which the Sovereign keeps the key. We saw the rest of the regalia, however, and very handsome it is, jewelled sceptres and swords, and royal state umbrellas and spears, and, as a reminder of not distant times, a case of poisoned Malay weapons. The palace is very commodious and beautifully situated, and contains an indifferent collection of British Royal portraits, and probably the most unrecognisable life-size portrait of W. E. Gladstone that man ever saw; doubtless the climate has affected those works of art. The present Sovereign is a very active young prince, greatly interested in his rubber plantation. He has a 120-h.p. Mercedes motor car, and thirty miles of admirable road on which to run it. The course must tend to become a little monotonous. The town is decidedly odd, for in its way it is a sort of Chinese Monte Carlo. "Fan-tan" is forbidden in Singapore, but Johore is independent, and so there are several establishments which are much resorted to, with "Gambling Farm" painted in English on their fronts. We saw some three Chinese open-air theatres, where plays with much clashing and noise were being acted by actors who appeared to have strayed out of Chinese vases as known to us at home; the plays were enacted on open stages about ten feet above the ground. The audience sit on the ground or stand. I presume a collection is taken at intervals.

I went one morning to the Law Courts of Singapore and heard the Chief-Justice deliver a considered judgment in a very intricate case as to certain rights in a property, the title to which it was admitted by both sides was a forgery. Courts at home are a trifle too warm for comfort; here the air was delightfully cool, for the Courts were great, wide, open halls, well shaded, and with many punkahs unintermittently waving. The Chief-Justice wore a gown but no wig; the members of the Bar wore no wigs, but as regards the upper portion of their persons they were otherwise immaculately correct in white ties, black waistcoats, and gown; but, without exception, they all wore white trousers, for the Law (which loves fiction even in the tropics) supposes lower limbs to be invisible. White, of course, is the universal dress of every European in this land. The newspapers are trenchantly written and interesting, and there can be little wanting to the happiness of those who can stand the climate, where turtle is the cheapest food and pineapples are a drug in the market. The present Governor is Sir John Anderson, an Aberdonian, who was long in the Colonial Office; he lives in a stately palace on a height above the town, and takes a vigorous and discriminating share in the administration of this happy little Colony, where, of course, there are many Scotsmen. Scotsmen, indeed, and men of Devon seem to share between them nearly all the positions of enterprise in the East, whether in the tea gardens of Assam, or the teak forests of Burma, or the tropical islands of the Malay Archipelago.

CHAPTER VII

CANTON AND MACAO

Hong Kong, March, 1907.

YESTERDAY I was in Canton, and to-day I am glad to be once more in this most un-Chinese, prosperous, cleanly, bright British Colony. Before we went into China proper, I should have said, "This is Chinese indeed." So it is in a sense, but there is a world of difference between Canton, a dirty, mediaeval city, and the stately buildings of the Colony. In Canton scarcely a street is wider than seven feet, and the only method of carriage is a sedan chair, and loads are carried on poles on men's shoulders. On every hand are shops, big and little, all open to the street, all with dangling signs in front, those signs being long narrow boards of red or gold, or any other colour, with the name of the shopkeeper in Chinese characters. Between swinging signs, along narrow ways, amid great crowds of pig-tailed, blue-gowned Chinamen, the visitor's chair makes but moderate progress, though the coolies have the will to trot fast enough if there were room. We visited the chief Confucian temple, dirty and undignified as so many Chinese temples seem to be. It is much resorted to on questions of health. There are some sixty seated figures; you select the one which represents your age, or that of the person you are interested in, and burn joss sticks before it, and pray. If your age is about sixty you begin again at statue number one; a very convenient arrangement, for thus by a polite Chinese fiction a prayer is equally efficacious whether it be addressed to No. 2 for children of two years of age or as representing veterans of sixty-two. Another way (as cookery books put it) is to take a sheaf of small bamboo slips and shake them about in a jar, towards the sacred figures, until one falls out of the jar. You examine it, and on it you find a number. You take that number to a neighbouring magic-physician and priest, whose counter is at your hand in the temple, and he hands you a folded paper which corresponds to the number; that paper tells the inquirer what is wrong with him, what caused it, and how he is to be cured. In this twentieth century in this vast city of the Chinese Empire this hanky-panky apparently rules the people's life. Near at hand is a more dignified Buddhist temple with "500 Genii," as they are sometimes called in guide books, all happy, seated figures, with a greater variety of expression and pose than the Kings at Holyrood, and resembling more nearly rows of bald-headed old benevolent bankers, as English tradition knows bankers at home, but all with a minimum of clothes and cross-legged. In this odd company is a statue of Marco Polo, of all people, and as he was the only one of the distinguished crew of whom I had ever heard, I stuck three little joss-sticks in the sand-jar in front of him, with the complete approval of the priest in attendance.

By various devious ways we shortly afterwards found ourselves at the place of public execution. When not so required it is a potter's field, and many half-baked pots stood on the ground. Against the wall were three or four large black crosses, on which the worst criminals are executed, but most lose their heads by a sword which was shown us, and the heads are preserved in jars. About 300 are said to be executed annually in Canton. I declined to look at the heads; it is a ghastly place to remember. Then we proceeded to the Temple of Horrors, where, with the pious view of frightening people into goodness, each chamber contains a graphic model of the sufferings to be endured in the Buddhist hell by the wicked; one is being crushed by an iron cap over his head, another is being boiled, a third is squeezed in a press, and so on. Each cell of this religious Madame Tussaud's has lifelike figures of a presiding judge at the back and attendant executioners of justice. Outside the bars sit a select congregation of fortune-tellers, a highly respectable and remunerative calling.

Then, upward, we went by the city walls—such walls!—to the Five-storied Pagoda, which is supposed to be more a fortress than a place of religion. There the mandarins meet to direct affairs when a war is in progress; and, if so, it explains a good deal. There are two huge statues, the God of War, of a ruddy countenance, and the God of Literature. They are seated side by side, and each has two attendants. In the intervals of their devotions to those big figures the mandarins survey the crumbling brick walls, with the rusted cannon, and think. What do they think about?

Perhaps their dead. It is highly necessary to build a suitable place of interment; if you can't do so in your life your relations may instal you in the mortuary, perhaps the pleasantest place in Canton, admirably clean, and gay with all manner of flowers and trees tortured into curious forms. There you can have your sealed and enamelled coffin deposited in a pleasant chamber, for which so much a year is paid. Before the coffin hangs a curtain; in front of the curtain, facing the entrance, is a table or altar on which a fresh cup of tea is placed three times a day. In some cases there is a handsome chair for the ghost to sit in while he takes his tea; in every chamber there are seats at the sides for mourners who wish to spend a quiet hour with their dead.

One could write much more on this singular city of Canton; so crowded with strong and healthy men, a city so dirty, men so ignorant, so absorbed in the contemplation of their own superlative merits. They seem well nurtured, they are industrious, they are incredibly numerous and prolific, they can live on next to nothing, they are not afraid of death. Are they to be the universal hewers of wood and drawers of water of the Far East, or is it to be as masters of all other races they are to spread over the earth? The latter is a terrible speculation for the white races; grant that in our time the yellow man may keep his place! It is not for a mere casual visitor to do more than note certain signs of the times.

Remarkable is the difference between the colonies of Europeans which impinge on this part of China. No colony could be more up to date in every way than Hong Kong, the great international port of the world. No place could be more somnolent than Macao, the ancient Portuguese Colony. Hong Kong is the mere ledge of a precipitous mountainous island, but the energy of our wandering race has scraped the hills so as to form terraces, on row above row of which a great city stands; nor has this been all, for now the foreshore has been dealt with, and imposing blocks of very high buildings of the most modern construction stand where a few years ago there was only a marshy shore, electric cars run along the level part of the town, and a mountain railway takes one to the fine heights of the Peak, a large expanse of moor-like mountain top where the finest residences of the merchants stand, commanding a glorious view of seas and islands. The shops are large and well stocked. There is a club of as noble proportions as any in Pall Mall. On every side there is evidence of prosperous trade and of a healthy place of residence alike for European and Chinaman; and the Chinaman is of course everywhere, and a respectable citizen he seems to be, and sometimes a very rich one.

The voyage to Macao takes about three and a half hours, through scenery which is varied and grand. Those great mountains might be on the shore of Loch Long. As a colony Macao is not a success by any means, but it is very beautifully situated, and no more charming retreat than this could be imagined for anyone who desires to leave the world very much behind. It is situated on a narrow peninsula, round which are an innumerable number of picturesque islands. On every side the eye is delighted with luxuriant vegetation and high mountains, and sparkling seas alive with innumerable varieties of junks. One side of the peninsula forms the landing place of the harbour; the other is laid out as a promenade by the water's edge, so that—but for the rickshaws—one might imagine oneself in Lucerne or Geneva, for the handsome buildings which fringe the road are purely Continental. The Portuguese have stamped the little town, over three centuries old, with the impress of the Old World. There are piazzas which might be found in some town of Central Italy; there are, too, such cobbly roads as only the Continent of Europe knows. But, unfortunately, there is next to no commerce, and the upkeep of the Colony is derived mainly from the license duty paid by the keepers of fan-tan gambling-houses—a game forbidden in Hong-Kong. Hundreds of gamblers travel every day to this Far East Monte Carlo. I use the word "hundreds" advisedly.

A mile or so out of the Colony—*i.e.* on the neck of the peninsula—one reaches a large arch and gate across the road; this is the Portuguese Custom-house; beyond it is half a mile of neutral ground, almost wholly used as a Chinese cemetery. Then you reach a bamboo gateway, and enter real China. Behind the gateway is a guard-house, and there the first person to greet us was a representative of the Imperial Chinese Customs in his shirt sleeves, who was, of course, the inevitable Scotsman, a Mr. Baillie, from Haddington. The value of Hong Kong trade annually is estimated at £50,000,000. In 1905 a total of 19,974 vessels of nearly 1,500,000 tons entered, and 18,416 vessels of 1,000,000 tons cleared with cargo, besides very many in ballast; probably it is now the largest shipping port in the world, and it possesses unrivalled steam communication to all the ends of the earth. The harbour has an area of ten square miles. The island itself has a circumference of twenty-seven miles, but the Colony includes a concession of 280 square miles on the opposite mainland and various islands. The population is about 300,000, of whom perhaps 11,000 are Europeans. Statistics as to Macao are not very clear, but the population is about 78,000, of whom some eighty are natives of Great Britain. The boundaries have been a subject of incessant negotiation between Portugal and China. The harbour is said to be silting up. Some tea, fire-crackers, tobacco, and preserves are exported. The Chinese, it must be remembered, use an enormous number of fire-crackers to frighten devils and otherwise. The contrast between Canton, an almost purely Chinese town; Hong Kong, Anglo-Chinese; and Macao, Portuguese-Chinese, is remarkable and instructive.

CHAPTER VIII

SHANGHAI AND FAR EAST

Miyako Hotel, Kyoto, Japan,
April 3, 1907.

I AM quite prepared to believe that in fine weather Shanghai is an imposing, beautiful, and cheerful city, but a week ago Shanghai was Glasgow at its very worst—wet, cold, misty, and muddy. As we came up from Woosung by launch from the "America Maru," the shores were grim and grey; tall stalks sent out black smoke to the murky air; the noise of factories and foundries was not absent; the water was discoloured as at the Broomielaw. In the streets the muddy coolies drew rickshaws through puddles, and roads were upturned for the completion of the electric tram car line. Carriages plied for hire—a departure from the habits of the Far East. The buildings are tall, and in some cases handsome, and the ground is so valuable as to command—especially on the river frontage—such prices as are usually associated with the city of London alone. Even our short visit was enough to show how great and remarkable is this European place of business set in the East. Anomaly of all anomalies, it is not British. There is only a British concession. Each nation has its own Consular Court, and there is much consequent inconvenience. The city is really, truly, and actually Chinese, and all the foreigners have is "conceded" rights.

We have now touched China at various points, and although it would be rash to express personal opinions, yet the impression may be recorded, due to conversation with residents in China of long standing, that the condition of many provinces of the great Empire of China must be intermittently one of liability to plague, pestilence, and famine. For this liability, it must be remembered, bad government is not specially responsible. The topography of China is such that a very large extent of country is absolutely flat. In the case of the sudden rising of a mighty river, there is no chance of escape for many an unhappy husbandman. If you live on a billiard table you must take the consequences. Every great devastation is necessarily followed by famine. Of course, with so prolific a population, the wastage of life is soon rectified, but a new disaster affects some other part of the Empire. What a problem in a hundred ways China presents! An enormous supply of much-needed, strong, honest labour is available, and yet the consensus of opinion of civilised European or American States appears to be for the moment that such labour should not be admitted where it is most wanted, and that for racial reasons only. The market for goods manufactured by the white man is thereby affected, for although China should be a most profitable field, the United States is practically boycotted at present. What the future may have for us will depend on the energy of our British merchants in making good use of their opportunities, but it was the view of a Shanghai merchant that if such a duty were put by us on foreign manufactured goods as would succeed in checking the importation of German goods into Great Britain, Germany would be forced to find foreign markets such as China to the great detriment of Great Britain, which is now by a long way the master of the Chinese market, (although Germany has already greatly strengthened her commercial position there). Fiscal reform demands of its students that they should take a wide sweep of the possibilities of British trade which has many aspects in the

Far East. To revert to Shanghai, there seems to be some apprehension locally that on the completion of the new electric car system there will be an outbreak of disturbance from dissatisfied jinrickshaw men, whose business will certainly be seriously affected. The occupation of a jinrickshaw coolie in Shanghai does not seem a delectable one at the best, but poverty in China is always very near the coolie. It is curious, by the way, to remember that this most convenient mode of conveyance has no greater antiquity at the very furthest than 1867, yet thousands upon thousands of men now depend on this human-pony-work for means of livelihood. I have travelled in many a strange way since coming East, but of all ordinary modes of progression the rickshaw is the quickest, cheapest, and cleanest.

It is to the landscape-gardening of a temple at Shanghai that we are said to owe the familiar willow-tree pattern of plate; before leaving Hong Kong we enjoyed the privilege of seeing the magnificent collection of the finest productions of Chinese ceramic and other art which Sir Paul Chater has lodged in a lordly pleasure-house on the Peak. The Salting Collection at South Kensington is more easily available to the Western world, but the Hong Kong amateur's collection is unique, and it is not the least of the many pleasures of a visit to Hong Kong to hear Sir Paul lovingly describe each beautiful object which once had its place in the Imperial Collection of Pekin.

We travelled from Singapore to Hong Kong in the "Zieten," a ship of the North German Lloyd, and from Hong Kong to Kobe in the "America Maru" of the Toyo Kisen Kaisha Line. On both ships scarcely a word of any language save English was spoken among the first-class passengers, for all the German passengers spoke English when not, of course, speaking among themselves. Why should German and Japanese ships be full of Englishmen? Put two questions—Is the supply of British ships inadequate? Do foreign lines afford superior attractions in the way of comfort? I am afraid the answer is "Yes" in each case. British ships by no means cater fully for the mighty Far Eastern trade; do the directors of our home lines note this? One hears it suggested that they should travel to the Far East themselves, or not add to their Boards any man who has not seen what they should have seen. The Far East is full of English life and energy and opportunities. It cannot be said that our home directors seem to realise this, or so much trade should not go in foreign bottoms. As to comfort, I must reluctantly own that foreign lines are more cleanly and more thoughtful for the comfort of travellers (so far as I have seen) than home lines. The nursery red-tape regulations of the "P. and O." are a by-word over the world—admirable ships and an autocratic way of treating passengers by, among other things, childishly irritating restrictions about trifles. The British India boats have captains who are courteous and approachable, but the cockroaches of which Rudyard Kipling speaks so tenderly in "From Sea to Sea" are a good deal too numerous (there may be specialities of cargo which account for something), and the departure from Calcutta, the arrival at Rangoon, and the departure from Rangoon when I was there, seemed to a landsman as badly managed and as uncomfortable as any tyrant could devise. On the German and Japanese boats there were neither mosquitoes nor cockroaches; there are few regulations, and the food is plentiful, well cooked, and varied. Why should we not put our house in order? No line, however excellently built its ships or courteous its commanders, can afford to slight the lessons of comfort and cleanliness which its rivals offer it. Curiously enough, the river lines, which have no rivals, seem to a traveller more unexceptionable than the ocean liners. The Irrawaddy Flotilla deserves and receives commendation from everybody, and the service on the Brahmaputra is quite adequate to the needs of those who sail up or down that mighty river. I have no special regard for the North German Lloyd, for the truth is the "Zieten" was overcrowded, and we were among the worst sufferers, but, apart from this, the conditions of travel as afforded by the line were deserving of commendation.

I date this letter from the ancient capital of Japan, but I am not going to write an account of Japan after only a very few days' stay. The anonymous author of an excellent little local guide supplied by this first-class hotel says with gratifying frankness—"There never has been a country about which so much absolute rot has been written by drivelling idiots, who have neither sufficient knowledge to make their works of value nor gift of language to make them readable." With this pungent warning in mind, let me only say that Japan is very cold indeed at present, and that this year's number of visitors is phenomenal and far beyond the capabilities of its few European hotels, if all tales be true.

CHAPTER IX

UP AND DOWN IN JAPAN

Miyanoshita, Japan, April 20, 1907.

"Japan is not in the tropics," says Murray's Guide sagely, and the visitor in April realises the truth of its warning. We sailed through the Inland Sea for the most part in rain, and though at Kobe we found things a great deal better, yet in Kyoto a fur coat was often very useful, especially on an excursion to the beautiful Lake Biwa, for although the sky was blue and the sun shining, the air was very cold. Kyoto was the capital of old Japan, the city of the semi-sacred Mikado, while the Shoguns really ruled the nation in his name for centuries at Yedo, now called Tokyo. Kyoto (in addition to the practical advantage of having a very excellent hotel) is full of such palaces and temples and gardens as no other city of the empire can show. And its shops! Like every other Japanese town, it is to all appearance a conglomeration of wooden huts (to say "hovels" is perhaps too strong), mostly of one story, very rarely of more than two. There are no shop windows to speak of; but enter one of the hundred marvellous repositories, and treasures of the most beautiful work in cloisonne, in pottery, in antique curios, and exquisite modern works delight the eye and empty the pocket. From Kyoto, too, many expeditions may be made. We went to Kameoka, and shot the rapids of the Katsura-gawa—a thrilling experience—and we spent a delightful day at the park-like Nara.

Japanese palaces in Kyoto and elsewhere are necessarily in some respects a disappointment, because, to begin with, they have externally few more architectural pretensions than other houses; a palace is simply a series of one-storied wood buildings, with apartments opening into and off each other by sliding partitions, and entirely void of furniture of any kind. The beauty and attraction lie in the fine mattings on the floor; the exquisite wood-work, the lacquer, the carvings, and the rare and valuable paintings. So, too, as regards the temples, whether Shinto or Buddhist. When you have seen half a dozen Japanese temples you have seen them all so far as the plan of construction is concerned, and it is simplicity itself. But as the eye becomes educated by the daily contemplation of shrine after shrine, here as in the palaces, is revealed the glamour of golden walls, the lacquer work which is unique in the world, the shrines on which an infinity of delicate workmanship has been expended. While it might be a hard saying that Japanese art cannot be appreciated out of Japan, it is true enough that to visit Japan gives one a more keen appreciation of the meaning of her art—an art which is essentially and entirely un-Western, which follows different ideals, and is intended to serve quite other conditions of life and modes of thought.

What is true of the buildings is not untrue of the gardens. Into their arrangement the Japanese have carried a sentiment which must be at least in some way guessed at (even if not fully appreciated) before they can be properly admired. To the English eye nothing can ever be more beautiful than an English rose garden in June. But that is very far from being beautiful *in excelsis* to the Italian gardener's eye. So, too, in Japan. The story is well known of the Englishman driving through his newly leased deer forest, and asking, "But where are the trees?" "Wha ever heard o' trees in a forest?" was the ghillie's scathing answer. So, too, if you ask a Jap, "Where are the flowers?" he may reply that you don't want flowers in a garden. Outside the east end of Kyoto is the country house of Ashikaga Yoshimitsu, built in 1479,—when he abdicated the Shogun's dignity,—and known as the Silver Pavilion. The garden is extraordinarily attractive, and yet on what does the eye first rest? On a curiously shaped heap of white sand, where Yoshimitsu, used to sit and indulge his aesthetic tastes; behind is another called the "Mound Facing the Moon," where he used to moon-gaze. The little rill is "the Moon-washing Fountain," and a stone in the tiny pond is "the Stone of Ecstatic Contemplation." The art of delicate adjustment of stones and water enters largely into the composition of those gardens, and an overpowering imagination which gives every object an aesthetic sense or value apart from what we should regard as its ordinary or primary value. Such a nation of aesthetes it was, which, a century after Yoshimitsu, saw the remarkable career of Sen-no-Rikyu, who was taken about by the great General of the day to preside at his tea parties in the intervals of battle, and who when he ultimately fell into disfavour and was ordered to commit harakiri, did so "in his tea-room after making tea, arranging a bouquet, and composing a Buddhist stanza." And such a nation of aesthetes it still is which travels long distances in very uncomfortably overcrowded railway carriages, or on foot, to see the cherry-blossom at Kyoto or Tokyo.

Yet it is this nation of sentimentalists who, on the other hand, have produced the remarkable canal, partly underground, which now connects Lake Biwa and Kyoto in the face of very serious engineering difficulties; which is building huge ships at Nagasaki; which has made Osaka into a Chicago eight miles square; which wears the ugliest European clothes with satisfaction, and imports German furniture for the modern Imperial palace. There is nothing too sentimental for the Japanese; there is nothing too prosaic.

From Kyoto we went to Nagoya, a flourishing city. It is not for its commerce the stranger goes to Nagoya, but to visit the remarkable castle, one of the wonders of Japan. It is not old; it was only built in 1610; it never was besieged. But it is far older than its date; it is a genuine early medieval stronghold of timber, built centuries after Europe had forgotten that such wood castles must have preceded all (or most) stone fortresses. There are huge stone walls as foundation; all else is timber, and the walls are 18 feet thick, and tier upon tier for five high storeys the keep rises; its gates are cased with iron; it is surrounded by a moat, and full within of ingenious devices for dropping burning metal on besiegers, and its walls are pierced with holes for arrows. On top are two golden dolphins, valued at £36,000. At Nagoya we went to the local theatre, where the ingenious revolving stage worked admirably and enabled the very pretty scenes to be promptly changed.

Next came a few days in the capital, a city of two million people, with their Sovereign living in a sort of island surrounded by a moat in the very heart of the place. It is a curious and pleasant thing in Japan that English is virtually the second language. Railway tickets are printed in English on one side; all railway notices are in English as well as Japanese, and in the interesting museums in Kyoto and Nara every article had its description given in English. Curiously enough, in Tokyo, where English newspapers are on sale everywhere, and English is the daily medium of communications between all foreigners (German or French or Italian) and the natives, English translations are not invariably affixed to the description of objects in the museums. From Tokyo we went to Nikko, of which the Japanese say "do not use the word magnificent till you have seen Nikko," and stayed at one of Japan's many most excellent foreign hotels. No Swiss hotels could be cleaner or better arranged, or with more varied table. Our innkeepers have a great deal to learn from the Japanese as to the art of making the stranger comfortable; and if only they would learn, it would be to their financial profit. Nikko is charmingly situated amid a wild and mountainous country, with the ever-present peculiarly clear and rippling water courses, of which the country has so many. The temples and tombs associated with the first and third Shoguns I must pass over, wonderful as they are as triumphs of national art; nor can I do more than mention the highway of ancient Cryptomerias, noble and magnificent as no other tree can be. Passing the sacred Red bridge one pleasant April morning we climbed upwards from Nikko, which is 2000 feet above the sea, to Lake Chusenji, which is about 2400 feet higher. The way is very difficult and steep, and when we reached the table-land, all the ground was thick with snow, on which the trees threw black shadows, for the sun was high in the blue sky. Through this curious blinding landscape we passed to the shores of the delightful lake which laps the foot of the sacred mountain Nantai-zan, which women are not allowed to ascend. Though the place was remote, the hotel has a telephone to Nikko, and there was nothing but commendation for the dainty lunch; had time permitted we should gladly have stayed there.

Next day from Nikko we made a journey by 'rickshaw, three trains, a private tramcar, and 'rickshaw again, for ten hours, to Ikao, which stands on a terrace on the north-east slope of Haruna-san, about 2700 feet above the sea. It is a favourite resort in summer, but on the 15th to 17th April we had the little hotel and its mineral baths all to ourselves. A grand view of high mountain ranges and great valleys is spread before the eye, and from Ikao one ascends to the still higher Lake Haruna, the site of an extinct crater. From a pass above the lake, and 1000 feet above Ikao, we descended to the far-hallowed temple, set amid a weird assemblage of fantastic gigantic peaks of rocks such as Gustave Doré drew in his illustrations to the *Inferno.* It is very appropriately dedicated to the Shinto God of Fire and Goddess of Earth, and even on the cold day when we were there many pilgrims came to pull the bell which hangs in front of the temple, to throw a few sen into the large box which receives money gifts, to kneel a few minutes on the steps in silent prayer, to clasp hands twice, and to offer a tiny parcel of rice. From a covered stage opposite the temple, a priest with a sort of bamboo fishing-rod received money in its split end, and returned to the pilgrims in the same manner a form of prayer, which was then offered at the altar steps, and on the stage at intervals an ancient priestess, on payment of ten sen, performed that sacred dance, with the "tokko" in hand, which means so little to us Europeans, and yet which is full of symbolic religion and teaching, for even the "tokko" itself symbolises the irresistible power of prayer, mediation, and incantation. The whole day's travelling was done on horseback, and sometimes the way was dangerous. Hazardous as sometimes were the Himalayan ways, and bad as was the Teesta road, they were as nothing to the breakneck paths and narrow ledges by the side of precipices along which our horses so wonderfully managed to keep their feet on this trip to Lake Haruna. The following day we travelled on to Myogi, having in our view for much of the time the smoking volcano of Asama. Myogi-san is a series of grand, sharp-pointed, deeply serrated dykes, whose highest summit is about 3880 feet. The effect of those arrow-like jagged peaks and ridges is extremely fine, and well worth the somewhat troublesome journey, but the ascent of the Daikoku-san, magnificent though it is, was a case of the roughest and wildest scrambling in a lonely land where accidents might be attended with the direst results. Fortunately we got back safe and sound to the little hotel of Myogi, which is purely Japanese. In its beautifully clean guest chambers, entirely empty of furniture, we took a Japanese dinner with chopsticks, seated in Japanese fashion, and we slept on the floor on Japanese quilts, and slept uncommonly well, too! Now we are in this lovely and famous Hakone district, two days' journey from Myogi, and it is raining cats and dogs, as only too often it does in Japan.

CHAPTER X

THE JAPANESE OF TO-DAY

Yokohama, 27th April.

WHAT about Japan and her trade? Japan is not simply a playground for tourists, a curio-shop for collectors. The world recognises her as a very serious force in the Far East. It is not possible for a passing traveller to arrive at opinions which may not be questioned, or which may not be vitiated by want of knowledge of some special kind. But we have seen a good deal of Japan up and down, and have read the daily admirable chronicle of Japanese life in the newspapers in the English language, of which there are so many. The advance of Japan has been wonderful; in the opinion of her people, her progress in the future will far outstrip the modest performances of the past.

But there is another side. Is Japan travelling too fast for her resources? Is she travelling in commercial unity with other nations? To the first question the answer undoubtedly is that Japan has not money to do all she wants to do. The European is not wanted as official or teacher in Japan, permanently. Let him teach what he knows; the Japanese can do as much as the foreigner can do whenever he has learned. And so he will. The Japanese engineer will design as well as the English engineer who taught him. The Japanese shipowner does not intend always to go to the Clyde for ships—witness the ships which are now building at Nagasaki. But if Japan is to execute all the mighty works which she contemplates, she must have money. Is the rest of the world going to give Japan money to enable her so to develop her resources that she may compete with Europe in the markets of Europe's merchants? For Japan by no means intends to manufacture only for herself. She is a born trader. China already is a large customer, and there are others. The meaning of Japan's manufacturing energy must be clearly understood so far as our Far Eastern trade is concerned.

Japan's aspirations have in the meantime rather outrun her abilites. There were disagreeable tales in Japan of banks which were, or had been, in difficulties. But the following cutting from the *Japan Daily Herald* of April 18, 1907, will serve to indicate something of the magnitude of Japan's trading ambitions since the end of the Russian war (a yen may be taken roughly at 2s.):

"According to the investigations of the Nippon Ginko, the capitalisation of new enterprises mooted during March aggregated Y70,337,400, showing a decrease to about one-fifth of the average capital required for the various new enterprises started during the last few months. The violent depreciation in the share market which set in since the latter part of January has had the effect of dampening the industrial fever, and several new enterprises schemed during the past months have had to be dissolved, while many more are in a state of suspension. It is believed that many new enterprises will drop through, the financial inactivity still continuing. The following are the new enterprises set on foot during March:

	Newly inaugurated.	Extension of business.
	Yen.	Yen.
Banking - - - - -	1,920,000	21,722,400
Spinning - - - - -	—	525,000
Electric - - - - -	—	200,000
Mining - - - - -	3,000,000	5,000,000
Aquatic products - -	2,100,000	—
Railways - - - - -	1,300,000	—
Manufacturing industries -	5,500,000	300,000
Insurance - - - - -	—	5,300,000
Trades, etc. - - - -	10,170,000	13,300,000
	23,990,000	46,347,000

This brings the total capitalisation for the new post-bellum enterprises up to Y1,566,004,530, of which Y1,107,149,180 is the amount involved in entirely new enterprises, while the balance is for the extension of businesses already existing."

The second question arises, is Japan travelling on terms of commercial unity with other nations? In other words is she a fair competitor? It is more easy to state the question than to answer it. The *Japan Advertiser*, in an interesting article, refers to "a thoroughly unworthy and un-American fear" in the United States that Japan is to be the States' most formidable commercial competitor, and says the fear must be due to "the rife and rapidly growing impression throughout the States that in some way or another Japan is not going to play fair in the great competitive struggle impending." "That it exists is undeniable, and it remains for Japan to show that it is unwarranted." Here I must leave the matter. The Chinese merchant has long had, and still has, an enviable reputation for integrity and fairness in the Far East, and it is to be hoped that the Japanese merchant in his haste to be rich will, nevertheless, prove himself to be possessed of the same characteristics. But China learned her European trade from generations of honourable traders. In feudal Japan trading was not an honourable calling, and when international trading was forced on Japan she was made the prey of most unscrupulous adventurers from the American side of the Pacific. Japan has therefore the two-fold disadvantage of no hereditary associations with the honest dealers of Europe and of having herself been tricked and beguiled before she knew her way about in commerce. She needs no teaching now. The *Japan Daily Mail* reports its native contemporary, the *Yorodzu Choho*, as printing the name of eight brokers of the Tokyo Stock Exchange as implicated in a plot for "deliberating, concocting, and spreading all sorts of alarming rumours" in the "bear" interest. They are said to have been responsible for the run upon the Asakusa Bank, and to have been "contriving a similar manoeuvre against the Tokai Ginko when their schemes were discovered." "The Tokyo police are now actively interfering, and so is the Department of Agriculture and Commerce, under whose jurisdiction the Stock Exchange falls."

The peril of Japan lies in her cleverness in adopting full civilised ways without the training which teaches how European ways (in trade as in other things) were arrived at. A friend gave me an amusing account the other day of a performance of "Hamlet" in Japanese which he had recently seen. Hamlet wore a frock coat and silk hat, and Polonius entered on a bicycle! The Japanese would see nothing unreasonable in that. Hamlet was a Prince of Denmark, and European Princes all wear frock coats and silk hats at Imperial garden parties. So, too, Polonius, as a trusted counsellor of State, would naturally have an up-to-date bicycle. This is a good illustration of the danger of importing European ways without having had time to understand the growth of things. Take, too, the hotels. The purely European hotels in Japan are as near perfection as they can be, for they are modelled on the best hotels of Europe. But the hotels which are half European and half Japanese are very bad; that is to say, the Japanese half is spotlessly clean, but the European half is apt to be most indifferent. The idea seemingly is that people who wear boots in hotels cannot be particular as to cleanliness, and consequently the rooms leave a great deal to be desired. In trade it is the same. The merchant who deals with the best houses of Europe will do business as they do it, adopting their ways in toto. But it is quite a different thing, obviously, when you have a native manufacturer pitting himself against a foreign manufacturer either in Japan (where the foreign manufacturer is in rapid process of being crowded out) or in markets open to both. In such cases the Japanese manufacturer has passed through no probation of the trade of centuries; he sees a thing is wanted, and he imitates it and supplies it; and there's an end on't. Devil take the hindmost, and I am afraid in that case the European is the hindmost. The surprising thing is that with all the Japanese cleverness in imitating European models, they apply no native taste to modifying European designs. Beautiful, indeed, are the products of Japan in things Japanese. But ugly, with an exceeding and unmitigated ugliness, are European articles manufactured by Japanese. This applies to art. The picture gallery in the Tokyo Exhibition is full of curious imitations of French and English artists. You can in a moment say "this is an attempt to paint after the manner of this or that European artist," but of real inspired painting in the European style there is very little indeed, and as to the portraits of men in European dress, they defy description.

The wages paid to women in Japan are very small, as will be seen by the following table, which I cut from a Yokohama newspaper (a sen is about a farthing).

Female Government Employees.

The number of female workers employed in the various Government establishments, and their daily average wages, are as follows:

Name of Establishment.	Number.	Wage Sen.
Printing Bureau - - -	1,405	25
Tobacco Monopoly Bureau -	11,930	16
Tokyo Arsenal - - -	3,120	32
Osaka Arsenal - - -	1,436	24
Senju Woollen Cloth Factory	1,247	21
Military Provision Depot -	48	39
Military Cloth Office - -	34	20
Naval Arsenal - - -	73	29
Naval Shimose Gunpowder Magazine - - -	22	23
Imperial Iron Foundry - -	9	22
Printing Office of the Department of Communications	30	22
Kobe Workshops of the Railway Bureau - - -	17	30

We made a delightful tour from Miyanoshita over the wild region where sulphurous fumes rise from the ground in all directions around us, and boiling water bubbles in pools at our feet, to the calm beauty of Lake Hakone, with Fuji (mostly in clouds) high above us. On the way down we stopped at a little village famous for its hot springs, and were invited to look into one pool under cover, where men and women and children were sitting together in steaming water. In another place about twenty persons of both sexes, entirely naked, were exposing their spines to the heating influence of a hot torrent in the open air. There was no indecency; there was simply nature, unashamed. But the spectacle could probably be seen in no other country in the world. At the end of Lake Hakone a boat awaited us, curiously rowed by standing rowers, and in it we went from end to end of the lake, then by chairs were carried by coolies over the high mountain passes until we had on our right the blue Pacific and the exquisite coast line of Japan, and on our left still looked down on Hakone. By a long but very beautiful road (if road it can be called that road was none) we reached Atami, on the Japanese Riviera; oranges were on the trees, while wisteria was in full bloom. The place is exquisitely beautiful. The following day we pursued the coast road, which is just as lovely as the Corniche road above Mentone, or more so, affording with constantly changing glimpses of bays and promontories, islands and fishing boats, rocky heights and leaping streams. Then by rail, and so at last to Enoshima, a singularly charming island, or, rather, peninsula, for only at high-water is it completely separated from the mainland. We spent the night again in a Japanese inn, and visited the cave of the dragon which Benten, the goddess, descended from the sky to marry, and thus effectually stopped his devastating ways. While we were in the great cavern an earthquake was taking place in Yokohama, and perhaps it is just as well in Japan not to go into deep caves, for an earthquake might close them for ever. The volcanic character of the country accounts for the bad roads in the mountains; constant seismic disturbances, and torrential showers cause landslips, large and small, very frequently, and they, of course, overwhelm the narrow paths. With all her civilisation, Japan has always Nature's forces to contend with to an extent undreamt of by the fortunate dwellers in the British Isles. From Enoshima we travelled to Kamakura, once the capital of Eastern Japan, but now a small place, yet remarkable above all other places in the land for the tranquil magnificence of the Daibutsu, or image of Buddha (in this case Amida). There are many such gigantic figures in Japan, but none more impressive amid its beautiful trees. Pictures give an idea of its size and position, but a perfectly inadequate conception of its calm, eternal majesty. We have seen nothing more absolutely beautiful in Japan.

Outside the gate is this inscription in English:

NOTICE.

Stranger, whosoever thou art, and whatever be thy Creed, when thou enterest this Sanctuary, thou treadest upon ground hallowed by the worship of ages.

This is the Temple of BUDDHA, and the gate of the Eternal, and should therefore be entered with reverence.

BY ORDER OF THE PRIOR.

Yesterday we were guests at the annual garden party "to view the cherry blossom" given by the Emperor to the Diplomatic Corps and the highest Japanese official society. The Emperor and Empress and their suite walked slowly through the gardens, and the guests fell in behind them and viewed the blossom. Then the Emperor took his seat in a pavilion, and numerous presentations were made to him. All ladies must wear European dress, and while many Japanese Princesses and ladies looked charming enough in their Parisian creations, it is but the truth to say that the Japanese woman always looks her daintiest and sweetest in her native dress. All men (except the Chinese Embassy) wore uniform, or frock-coats and silk hats, the latter the ugliest costume in the world under certain circumstances. After the presentations came refreshments—Moet and Chandon's champagne, and turkey, and all things European. The scene was very animated and picturesque in that Imperial garden of white cherry blossom and pink peach blossom, with its pretty lake and beautiful view of the blue sea. We were fortunate enough to end our visit to India as guests at the Viceroy's State ball in Calcutta, and we are fortunate, too, in saying farewell to Japan at the Sovereign of Japan's most typical and fascinating garden party.

CHAPTER XI

SAN FRANCISCO AND MONTEREY

We arrived at San Francisco from Yokohama by the Union Mail steamer *Mongolian*, an American-built ship. It was her thirteenth voyage; she sailed on a Friday: she ran aground leaving 'Frisco on her outward trip; she ran on a rock in the Inland Sea of Japan; she had a case of smallpox, which necessitated quarantine at Yokohama. But, despite those depressing things, she got safely to port with the largest number of saloon passengers ever brought from the Far East to California. It cannot be said that the table was good, and the crew of Chinese and mongrel nationalities did not impress one favourably, nor was civility (which is common alike to British, German, and Japanese ships) apparent on this American ship. The voyage was calm, but quite uninteresting, for on the Pacific day succeeds day with nothing seen save sea, and sea, and yet more sea. The stop at Honolulu was a delightful change. The Sandwich Islands are exquisitely beautiful, the hotels are good, the climate perfect. Where else in the wide world can one bathe in a sea as sparkling as that before the Moana Hotel? Where can one watch, astonished, such startling, wonderful, iridescent fish as in the little Aquarium? Where, elsewhere, does the cactus grow into such great gnarled trees? The native is in course of rapid disappearance, and the Japanese and Chinese have taken his place. Some hundreds of Portuguese settlers have been brought in to counterbalance the Asiatic immigration.

From the sea San Francisco does not appear a stricken town, for the fire did not affect its water front. When you emerge from the Custom-House shed, however, the awful spectacle defies description. Four square miles of business city were swept by fire, and those four square miles are covered with heaps of ruins to this day, with here and there, by rare exception, a great slim sky-scraper rising like a commercial lighthouse out of the dismal surroundings. India has miles of forgotten dwellings around Delhi, and Amber, near Jaipur, Fatehpur-Sikri, near Agra, and Chitor are all abandoned cities centuries old, but all of them time has benignantly touched, and the white marble temples and beautiful towers which survive make one forget the dead civilisation. Luxuriant vegetation covers all that was mean, or it has crumbled to earth. But San Francisco in its ruins is stark, staringly modern, pathetically ugly. It was not the earthquake which did the mischief—at least not directly—a few million dollars would have rectified all the harm the earthquake did, and it providentially happened at an early hour in the morning before domestic fires were lit, otherwise the mischief would have been still greater (for 95 per cent. of all the chimneys fell). But after the earthquake came the fire, and the water supply was so unfortunately arranged that the earthquake put it entirely out of gear, with the result that the fire once lit could not be extinguished. Then dynamite was used to blow up buildings in advance of the flames, and, so mad were all men that, it is said, dynamite was freely used where it was quite superfluous; thus it came about that where earthquake and fire failed to destroy, dynamite added a third cause of ruin. Fortunately the sea front was safe, and so was the city of Oakland across the bay, which is as Birkenhead is to Liverpool. The energy of the citizens would very soon have raised a new San Francisco. Unfortunately their public spirit has been paralysed. The municipality is involved in a complicated tangle of "graft," bribery, and dishonesty. Americans who prize municipal purity when they can get it (but they do not seem to expect it) might have stood even the dreadful state of municipal corruption, and gone on rebuilding San Francisco, but Labour now stepped in with such demands that all enterprise was virtually throttled. In May, on our arrival, the tram car men were on strike, and in sympathy with them the masons and builders threw bricks and "rocks" (*i.e.* stones) from the walls of houses in course of construction at and on the few cars driven by "scabs," regardless of the danger to innocent passers-by. Passengers were followed up on leaving a car and assaulted, sometimes to the point of death, or they were traced to their homes, and inquisition made as to what influence could be brought to bear by threats to deter them from travelling by car. The cement workers passed a resolution imposing a fine on any of their body who travelled by car. The barbers refused (in instances) to shave a passenger who alighted from a car. Bombs were placed on the car track and on cars; lumber and rails and piles of brick were set in the way, stones were freely thrown at motormen, and a sailor who ventured to say that though he was a "Union sailor" he was glad the cars were running, was set upon at once by half a dozen men and struck senseless by a terrific blow from a cleaver.

"When the ambulance from the Harbour Emergency Hospital arrived, the place was deserted except for Bowling, who lay in a pool of blood upon the floor. At the hospital Dr. Roche pulled several pieces of bone and a collection of other foreign bodies from the man's head." Yet bear in mind that San Francisco is a city of such immense distances and steep hills that unless workpeople use cars they cannot get to their places of employment. As cars did not try to run after dark for many days, shopkeepers and offices closed about five o'clock that the employees might get home as best they may. The well-to-do were not much better off. There are few cabs, and the drivers charged two dollars and a half (say ten shillings) to go from the Custom House to a hotel. Motor cars were used by private owners, but to hire one cost £10 sterling a day. Further, the telephone girls were on strike; the postal service was very irregular; all the laundries were on strike, and one could get nothing washed, so that some restaurants used paper table covers instead of linen. The police appeared to do nothing to repress disorder. Contractors could not make any binding arrangements either for clearing away rubbish or erecting new buildings, as at any moment the workmen might demand fresh terms. The result was anarchy of the worst kind.

While things are as we saw them, it is useless for capitalists to put money into restoring San Francisco. The shops have migrated to Van Ness Avenue, which is very much as if Argyle Street and Buchanan Street shops were re-erected in wooden shanties in front of Kew and Grosvenor Terraces, while all eastward to the Broomielaw remained a wilderness of dusty, broken-up streets, with ruins and rubbish on every plot which once was the site of a business block. It is sometimes said the hotels are just as they were. This is not so. The Fairmount Hotel is a magnificent building, like the Carlton in London; it was finished before the fire, and burnt out but not otherwise destroyed; it was opened in May, but only 100 of its 500 rooms were ready; also, owing to the car strike, it was practically inaccessible except by motor car or its own omnibus. The Palace Hotel, once an enormous building, is represented by a very modest country-looking inn, where we stayed in most suburban quiet, though it is in the very heart of the former city. The St. Francis is a collection of wooden sheds opposite the great hotel which is to be. Had the Labour leaders recognised that here was a chance for good wages for a long period for thousands of men, San Francisco would to-day have been something very different from the appalling city it is. They are said to have made enterprise impossible and destroyed trade; and if trade unions frighten away the money-spender, what use is the union to the workmen?

With things as they are in San Francisco everyone was anxious to get away as soon as possible, and we travelled to Del Monte, 100 miles southward on the Pacific Coast. There was constant sunshine, gardens with flowers of every shade and perfume, and laundrymen who consent to work (with mighty high remuneration). Close at hand is Monterey, the original capital of California, revered for its ancient buildings. One realises on visiting them that antiquity, after all, is a thing not of centuries but of circumstances. A rickety timber cottage is much reverenced because it was the first house of the kind in Monterey, built in 1848 with lumber brought from Australia; the first theatre of California, built shortly afterwards, is also an archaeological remnant; it is a shed somewhat resembling the sheds built at Heligoland at the time of the Crimean War for the then enlisted Foreign Legion (who were never sent to the field); but the Monterey theatre has this added interest, that here Jenny Lind sang. Near at hand is the house where Robert Louis Stevenson lived, and where he married. The inscription painted on the front, "R. Stevenson House," does not convey much to the travelling Scot without local explanation. At Carmel, a few miles away, is the Mission del Rio Carmelo, founded in 1771, and in Monterey itself is the San Carlos Borromeo Mission Church of 1770. Scarcely ancient are those days in Scotland, but they are fragrant with remote historical associations to Californians. There are 136 acres of garden and forest in the hotel grounds, with lake and golf course and maze, and a ranch eighteen miles away up in the mountains also owned by the hotel. There was nothing in this lovely corner of the earth which did not minister to the delight of all the senses, and yet even here the unfortunate San Francisco labour troubles reached out a retarding hand. Newspapers did not arrive until nearly one o'clock, sometimes long after. The Southern Pacific Railway offers, on paper, a great variety of trains to and from San Francisco, yet a notice in the hotel hall politely asks guests to travel by a train leaving here at 8 a.m.—"all other trains are subject to transfer or great delay, and should not be used except when absolutely necessary and the inconvenience is thoroughly understood in advance."

When we travelled in the Yosemite Valley

a few days later we were shown the place where all the stage coaches one day last year were stopped by one masked robber and the passengers forced to hand over their valuables. It seemed incredible. Yet in June this year, shortly after we left California, the same thing happened again at the same place. Running north to Portland, Oregon, a wooden trestle bridge over a gully took fire, and our train was detained for twenty-six hours at a little village until a new one was built, and we have had many other uncomfortable reminders of how dangerous railway travelling in America is. In the first five months of 1907 thirty-eight serious railway accidents occurred in the United States, and 273 persons were killed and 925 were injured. Is it wonderful that there should be serious accidents if the position of matters in New York State is typical; here, in the first four months of this year the number of broken rails removed from tracks was 836, the failure being principally in rails recently rolled. The *New York Times* suggests as a remedy the removal of the import duty on rails, so that the competition of foreign manufacturers should induce the Steel Trust to improve the quality of its rail output. But bad rails are not the only cause of accidents on American railroads.

A tour in America is made pleasant by the unstinted hospitality and kindness of friends in the cities where one stays, but the practical inconveniences of life in the west of the great Republic are so numerous that one may be pardoned for thinking that the travelling American who criticises Scottish ways conveniently forgets a good deal of the discomfort he lightly endures at home.

CHAPTER XII

MISSIONS IN INDIA

I WAS asked to act as a delegate to the General Assembly of the Presbyterian Church of India from the Foreign Missions Committee of the General Assembly of the Church of Scotland (of which Committee I was not a member) along with the Rev. the Hon. Arthur Gordon, then acting Chaplain of the Church at Simla; but I was not charged with any duty of visitation or inspection of missions, and I knew none of the missionaries personally. My observations are therefore only those of a fresh inquirer, and subject to correction by those who know better than I.

We must remember in going to visit missionary fields that although the days of missionary hardships are not past, yet the missionary in India, at all events, does not, as a rule, either war with beasts nor run the risk of being beaten with rods or imprisoned. In some aspects the life of the

Indian missionary is just as monotonous and void of excitement as that of any man in our midst.

Hegesippus, who cannot have died later than A.D. 192, tells us how the grandsons of Jude, the brother of our Lord, were sent to the Emperor Domitian, who examined them as to their land and money. For land, they said they had only 39 acres and cultivated it themselves, and they showed their hands, and their worn bodies as proofs of their real character of ordinary hard-working men. This is, in a sense, what we must say of our missionaries; they are ordinary men; no halo surrounds them; theirs is the common round, the daily task; their possessions are small, and their trials are written in their flesh.

The home attitude to Missions has within my own time taken three distinct aspects. Very many of us were brought up on the missionary literature which dealt largely with the horrors of the car of Juggernaut, suttee and so forth. All Indians were ignorant heathens and it was the duty of boys and girls at home to subscribe to enable missionaries to bring civilization and humanity to them. A very marked change followed upon the lectures of Max Müller, and the publication of the sacred books of the East, and especially among reading men there was a direct movement to the opposite extreme. We were told that the philosophy and the learning of the East were the best adapted for Eastern peoples; that every nation really had the religion that suited it best; that caste was after all little more than a trades-union, and that Christianity only made useless native Christians. A third phase we have now reached. We recognise all the merits of Eastern philosophy, but so far as the practical life of the people is concerned that high philosophy has little influence. The essence of Hinduism is veneration of local deities; the superstition is as gross as the old missionaries told us; there is urgent need for wise missionary effort which, while recognising the high ideals of Hindu Mahometan and Buddhist in their philosophies, goes direct to the root of the matter in the daily life of the people. It may be said, generally, that all modern missionary effort in India is conciliatory, educative and beneficial. How far it leavens the whole lump is a great question on which missionaries may not be the best authorities, absorbed as they are each in his own sphere of influence. The government of India is a Christian government, but it wisely exerts no influence which would be felt as oppressive by the millions, who, sincere in their own faiths (as they understand them or misunderstand them), would be roused to the bitterest antagonism by government compulsion.

The country is more or less allocated among the Churches for missionary effort. Thus the Church of Scotland is in evidence in the Punjab, Poona, Madras, and at Kilimpong (touching almost Thibet, Bhutan, and Independent Sikkim).

Central India is largely a field of the Canadian Church. At Ahmedabad I visited the flourishing Church of the Irish Presbyterian Mission. At Udaipur, in the native State of Mewar, Dr. Shepherd's mission is maintained by the U.F. Church. He has worked there for many years. His church was filled in the morning at the Hindi service, and his evangelists go into the bazaars in the afternoon and repeat his sermons. In the evening he reads the service of the Church of England and preaches in English. I read the Lessons for him.

It is curiously indicative of the varied nature of missionary effort in India, that while at Ahmedabad the converts live in a separate village; in Udaipur the Christians live among the pure Hindus.

I arrived at Indore in December to attend the third Assembly of the Presbyterian Church in India. Nearly all the Presbyterian Missionary agencies of

Scotland, England, and Canada are united. The union is more religious and mutually helpful than incorporative. Each Church's missionaries are still legally responsible alone to the Church which sends them out, but the true teaching of Presbyterianism as to the equality of all in the work of the ministry, with the necessary accompaniment of mutual helpfulness, is well brought out by the union. There was never, of course, any real diversity between the belief or the objects of the missionaries, and "union" here is certainly strength.

The Assemblies of the Presbyterian Church cannot be attended, as are our own Assemblies, by clergymen from all the country, for the distances are great and money is scarce; but on each occasion a large number of men are brought together for religious and social purposes who otherwise would know very little of each other. I understand the Assembly of 1905, at Nagpore, was largely a U.F. missionary gathering, and the Assembly of 1906, at Indore, certainly was largely a Canadian missionary gathering. The meetings were held in the large, cool, Bronson hall.

Dr. Youngson, of the Church of Scotland's Mission at Jammu, was the Moderator in 1905, and in 1906, by a vote, a native pastor of Bombay,

Mr. Nakombi, was elected Moderator. With Dr. Graham, of Kalimpong, by his side as Clerk of Assembly, his duties were made light, and it was an impressive sight to see men of such diverse races willingly met under the presidency of a native minister. The delegates from other Churches received a hearty welcome from a large meeting, and addressed the Assembly. The representatives of the Church of Scotland were as already mentioned the Rev. the Hon. Arthur Gordon, B.D., and myself. The Presbyterian Church of Canada was represented by the Rev. R. P. MacKay, D.D., secretary of that Church's Mission Committee. The opening meeting was also addressed by the Right Hon. Samuel Smith, formerly member for Liverpool, and Mr. William Jones, M.P. for Cardigan. The representatives of the United Free Church, Sir Alexander Simpson, M.D., and his son, the minister-elect of Cove United Free Church, arrived on Saturday evening. On Sunday there was a large attendance at a Hindi service at 8 a.m., and at 9 a.m. Mr. Gordon preached to a crowded congregation, many of whom from year's end to year's end as a rule hear no discourses but their own, and then almost without exception in some native tongue. At three o'clock Holy Communion was celebrated. A number of Scotch, Canadian, and native ministers took part, and the officiating elders were Sir Alexander Simpson and the Right Hon. S. Smith.

From Indore, Mr. Gordon, my wife and I visited Russelpura, an industrial mission under the charge of Mr. Cock, formerly of Klondyke, for the training of native boys whose parents died of famine. Owing to the strong Indian feeling of caste, men dying of famine would often rather perish than receive food from any one but a Brahmin, but in the case of the poor orphan children, who were saved from starvation, the Church has some hopeful material. The mission is conducted with great wisdom. The children live as other Indian children do, in the simplest way. They sleep most of the year in the open air, and eat the ordinary native meals. They learn simple arts of weaving, carpentry, etc., in order that they may go forth in life equipped with the best sort of skill for procuring their livelihood in the villages. A ready market exists in London for all they can produce. And *more.* And herein lies one of the difficulties of such a mission. Is it to become an industrial centre for the supply of Indian goods to England, in which case it must grow enormously and the workers be retained into manhood, and a small town be allowed to go up, or is it to remain a training school, a native technical college? The temptation to increase the revenue for general missionary purposes by accepting home orders on an extensive scale is great; on the other hand, the whole benefit of the scheme would be imperilled so far as the missionary influence is concerned of the boys themselves when going into native villages. On the whole the sensible men who govern the mission are disposed to keep Russelpura strictly to its benevolent and educational purposes, and the Church will not be lost in the manufactory.

I had not intended to go further north than Lahore, but we were very strongly urged by Captain Charteris of the Bengal Sappers, a nephew of the Rev. Dr. Charteris, to visit him at Rawal Pindi, and we arrived there on Saturday, 29th December, and as there was a case of enteric fever in Captain Charteris's bungalow, we became the guests of Mr. Roche, the Church of Scotland Chaplain to the troops. On Sunday morning we attended service at the English military church—a beautiful and spacious building—and in the evening we attended the Presbyterian service. A former Lieutenant-Governor of the Punjab caused at certain stations, small houses to be erected called Prayer-rooms for the use of those who might desire to retire to meditate. Such a hall is all the Church of Scotland has at Pindi; the Government have undertaken to give a site for a proper church, and certain difficulties having arisen as to the site, it was to view it that Captain Charteris had pressed me to visit Pindi. There can be no doubt the site is one of the best in Pindi, and I am glad to say the church is now to be built. We Scotch are a long-suffering race as regards church facilities for our Scottish soldiers in India. I confess I cannot understand our patience. The next station of the Presbyterian Church which I visited was at Darjeeling, in the Himalayas, where Mr. Kilgour is missionary, with Mr. H. C. Duncan and Mr. Arthur Tulloch, assisted by their wives and four native ordained missionaries, fourteen native catechists, and thirty-five Christian teachers. There are rather less than 1000 native Christians in thirteen stations, and fifty-five schools with about 1800 scholars. Several of the catechists are supported by congregations and Sunday schools at home at a cost, it is said, on an average of £20 a year for each. The Goorkha Mission to Nepal is carried on by the Darjeeling native Christians themselves, and this is a very happy sign. It was pleasant to hear at the Indore Assembly that several of the native churches represented there were also actively engaged in evangelical work at their own cost. Unless this is done, Christianity is in danger of remaining an exotic in India. At this point I must explain how this is more precisely. It must be remembered that Christianity is not the only converting Church; on the contrary the Mahommedans are very earnest proselytisers. In many respects it is impossible to deny the purity of their creed as compared with village Hinduism and its confusion of native powers. The Mahommedan has many advantages over the Christian. He is a man of like physical frame and the like modes of thought as the Hindu, and he can clinch his argument very effectively by such an appeal *ad hominem* as this: "If you become a Mahommedan, I will give you my daughter in marriage." This he will certainly do. The Christian—if a European—can only say: "And when you are a Christian, you will be my brother." But after all it is only a quasi-fraternal link, for the white man and the black must for ever remain separated, so far as social life is concerned; it is against nature that the races should intermarry. If, therefore, native Christians will themselves become missionaries, and support missionary efforts, they are able to deal with social problems much more successfully than we can. The white man living in a white man's house, wearing white man's clothes, going "home," sending his children "home," may be a teacher and a friend, but he can never get to the heart of things as the native can.

The Darjeeling mission works among many races, but it is well to remember that it is also one of our strongest posts of Presbyterianism in India. The Church of Scotland is in no back water in a place where three successive Governors of Bengal have been among the regular congregation during the summer season.

From Darjeeling we travelled to Kalimpong; no easy journey. The landscape was glorious in the extreme. We were travelling on narrow paths cut in the side of great mountains, amid an impressive and awe-inspiring silence; occasionally a great bird floated in the air of the vast valleys by which we passed; otherwise all was silence. Not a breath stirred the branches, not a bird's note was heard. The first night we rested at Pashok, at the house of Mr. Lister, a tea planter, who gives a cordial welcome to all friends of Dr. Graham. Here I had a slight recurrence of fever from which I had already suffered in Calcutta before leaving for Darjeeling, and was in bed all the time we stayed in Pashok. The next morning, however, we were again on the road, and by the afternoon we saw the Church of Kalimpong on its height. It strongly recalls a Scottish village church of the best type. The ascent is long and trying, but we received a warm Scottish welcome from Dr. and Mrs. Graham. What is known as the Guild mission, Kalimpong and Dooars, has 2700 native baptised Christians in 23 stations. There are 39 schools with 1100 scholars. The Bhutan Mission is carried on by the Kalimpong native Christians themselves. While we were at Kalimpong the death of Mr. Edward Taylor, of the Universities Mission, on Christmas day, 1906, was yet recent. He died in the Dooars of black water fever, a true martyr of the Church. He was greatly beloved. The schools at Kalimpong are supplemented by technical teaching, and it is pretty to see the native girls learning to make lace. While we were there they were making the lace for the gown of the Moderator, Dr. Mitford Mitchell. I trust they may make the lace for successive Moderators. Working with those gentle, clever native maidens were two of the little girls of Dr. Graham's family. A Women's Industries House for girls from a distance, and to provide a residence for the ladies in charge, is wanted. It will cost £1000 to build and finish. Government will give £600. The other

£400 will be found at home. There is an excellent infirmary, the beds in which were presented by various Scottish parishes, as notices above the ends testify. Tibetans who are injured now know their best course is to come to Kalimpong, and many a strange visage we saw above Scotch bed-clothes. Besides Dr. Graham, there are at Kalimpong a medical missionary and a lay evangelist to the Tibetans, nine ladies, two ordained native missionaries, twenty-four native evangelists, sixty Christian teachers, and five medical dispensers. Dr. Graham oversees the whole large establishment, has monthly meetings with the various teachers, and goes round visiting the native stations. The St. Andrew's Colonial Homes at Kalimpong are given in the year-book as under this mission, but they are not strictly speaking Presbyterian missions. What to do with Eurasians, *i.e.* the children born of white fathers and native mothers, is one of the direst of the minor problems of the East. Those unfortunate children are only too likely to be neglected, while they particularly require judicious care. They are looked down on by the pure whites, and they, themselves, hold themselves immeasurably superior to the brown race. They are apt to have the faults of both races and the virtues of neither. They don't want to work, and they have no means of maintaining themselves decently without work. Dr. Graham, six or seven years ago, founded the St. Andrew's Colonial Homes at Kalimpong, where in eight cottages some two hundred children are now being trained in habits of self-reliance and order. Each house has its "Auntie" and her assistant, and no servant of any kind is employed. The boys must do their own work, besides going to school. In one house was an excellent lady from Aberdeenshire, who had acquired thorough training in Dr. Barnardo's homes. A pile of Aberdeen newspapers was in a corner, and from it I gleaned a good deal of interesting information as to an approaching election in the South Division of Aberdeen in which, at the time, I had some personal interest. In another were a husband and wife from Airdrie. There is a capital teacher of joinery and similar crafts, and a good agricultural superintendent. Here, far lifted from all ordinary temptations and in a pure and healthy atmosphere, those neglected children are brought under the best influence, and it is pleasant to know that nineteen of them are now being trained on board H.M.S. "Southampton" at Hull for the Royal Navy which others have already entered. The Homes are supported by

Scotsmen and Englishmen all over India, and are not sectarian in any way. They are purely benevolent, but the wise and simple government is that of Dr. Graham and the Guild Mission. At Kalimpong is also the headquarters of the Training Institution of the Universities Mission, founded in 1886, and supported by the University Association of the four Scottish Universities and St. Cuthbert's congregation, Edinburgh. The particular field of work is Independent Sikkim. The Institution buildings are quite new, and were built to the designs of Mr. Taylor, who did not live to teach in them. Besides the missionary specially maintained by St. Cuthbert's, there are eight catechists and nineteen Christian teachers. In the Institution there are some thirty students. Under the superintendence of the mission are nineteen schools with 350 scholars, and the native Church in the assigned field of work is said to contain 305 baptised Christians in eight stations.

I emphasize *baptised* Christians. One of the greatest difficulties in obtaining support to Indian missions is the allegation commonly made that Christian servants are bad servants, and that native Christians, as a rule, are a bad lot. For two and a half months we had a servant, a Madras Roman Catholic, and a more honest or straightforward and willing servant no one could have. Every article in my luggage was known to him, and nothing ever went missing in his hands. Dr. Graham told me that, hearing again and again of the bad character of the Christians employed in tea-gardens in the Dooars, he made a personal census of the Christians employed there. Of all the "bad lots" he found only two were baptised Christians. The others were either men of the lowest castes who had adopted the name of Christian to give them a spurious rise in the world, or men who had been expelled from higher castes for serious reasons, and who adopted "Christian" as a caste name which barred inquiry. Therefore, when you hear the native Christian disparaged, ask your informant if he personally knew the man whose character he speaks badly of, and if he ascertained whether the man had really any right at all to be called a Christian. It is sometimes said by the apologist for the bad Christians that the example of our countrymen in India is such that they regard Christianity as little more than a social brand associated with the dominant race. If this means that the British in India are not all active missionaries, it is true, but if it means that the British in India set, as a rule, a bad example to the native, it is emphatically not true. All the virtues of the English in India are

Christian virtues—not that they are the monopoly of Christianity in theory, but that in practice the English in India are the active practisers of Christianity in the largest sense—they are strictly just, they are honourable, they are humane. The word of a Sahib is honour itself with the natives. But what about a Sahib's vices? As regards drunkenness, it is enough to say that the white man who drinks immoderately in the heat of India has already dug his grave. India is no place except for the clean-living European. Individual exceptions only prove the rule. If there is occasionally drunkenness or other fault on the part of the British soldier, it is due to want of a little elementary physiological teaching at home and the human frailty of the young soldier. The Indian native is no fool, and I should be extremely surprised to hear that he judged Christianity by the very occasional individual lapses of an extraordinarily well-behaved body of young men.

We visited many other churches in India, and met missionaries and clergymen of all denominations. In Calcutta I was able to pay only one visit to the General Assembly's College, where the best secular education is given and religious instruction in Bengali and English. There is a house of residence for students. I visited the

Women's Mission at Bow Bazaar with Miss Mungle, one of its heads. The house is delightfully spacious, but unfortunately it is not the property of the mission, who have been required to remove. There are eight Hindu schools, with about a thousand scholars, taught by thirty native Christian teachers and two Hindu pundits. Many Zenanas are visited for Bible-reading and hymn-singing only, while in over seventy houses secular teaching is also given.

The work of the Church of Scotland and other Churches in India is not to be judged by one who has only been a few months in India, but it is possible to form a definite opinion as to the needs of all evangelising agencies. Missionaries should be young, and thoroughly sound in health. The case of young women who marry young missionaries is full of danger. They may be far from medical aid at their most trying times; they will quite certainly be without many of the ordinary comforts of home, and subject to a thousand discomforts incident to Eastern life. Their young children must go home. They themselves will incur expense going backwards and forwards. It is true a wife may be the greatest of helpmates to a missionary, but I am not sure that over all a celibate missionary class is not the best; there is however a native preference for married men. To organised settlements like Kalimpong where ladies have every comfort my remarks do not apply. Missionaries, should be most thoroughly imbued, not only with the spirit of Christianity, but with that exhibition of it which is enforced in the apostolic injunction, "Be pitiful; be courteous." Nowhere is intolerance so offensive as when it may chance to be exhibited by a Christian minister in a land like India. The religions of the Hindu and the Mahommedan, the Sikh and the Buddhist, are great powers for good. Theirs is the moral standard of millions of men. By their guidance they lead upright and honest lives, according to the measure of instruction which has been given them. The partial revelation of God which such religions give is not a matter for gibe or joke. A missionary should be a man with the widest possible knowledge of the faiths he proposes to supplant, and should as rapidly as possible acquire the vernacular. To teach Christianity through the medium of English alone is a slow, slow job. Tolerance, fairness, comprehension, sympathy, are necessities. European clothes are no necessary part of Christianity, either for teacher or taught. But it is very difficult for the missionary to abandon not only kindred and friends, but also his modes of life and the costume which marks him as one of the dominant race. I do not judge; I am in no position to do so; but for all the reasons I have given I urge again that the hope of Christianity in India lies in its native clergy, who are men of the like habits with their people, and therefore the missionary educational work which fits earnest, self-convinced natives to be themselves apostles to their brethren is of the very highest service.

I am not blind to the fact, that if the object to be attained is an entirely native Church, it does not follow that the native Church will not take forms different—it may be widely different—from Presbyterianism at home. Neither the theory of Presbyterian government, nor its practice in modern Scotland (nor indeed congregational worship) are allied to Indian ideas, but those are problems of the future; of their existence we are warned by the various transformations of the theistic movements associated with the once famous name of Keshub Chunder Sen, and by the manner in which the native Christians of Madras have—very much against the wish of the Roman Church—developed a caste of their own. (Our own Christianity as an Eastern religion has taken forms in the West of Europe widely different from the gathering of the saints in Jerusalem, or the groups of believers to whom Paul, a Semitic Roman citizen imbued with Greek philosophy, addressed his pastoral letters.) In this connection I must remark in passing upon the influence exercised by Mrs. Besant and the Theosophists of the Central Hindu College at Benares, which is, perhaps, as yet little appreciated in Britain. It is a curious fact that two women, Mrs. Eddy in America and Mrs. Besant in India, should unquestionably be the religious teachers of the widest influence in the modern world. The effort of the teachers is to teach pure Hinduism instead of corrupt village Paganism. The view taken by missionaries of the work of the College is not uniform. Some regard it as mischievous, since it is non-Christian; others, with whom I range myself, regard with favour every movement adapted to native modes of thought which makes for the better spiritual life of the people, *i.e.* which puts doctrine before ceremonial, and the search for truth before simple satisfaction in temple worship, often intensely degrading. A recent number of the *Hibbert Journal* puts very clearly the importance of a deep study of this Theosophical movement, which appeals keenly to the intensely metaphysical mind of the educated Indian. We do not know that at its best this movement may not, indirectly but ultimately, lead to Christianity, as being far more satisfying than Theosophy, and at its worst—even its bitterest opponents admit that its apostles are teachers of pure and earnest minds, and that it is better to be a good Hindu than a bad Hindu. With the singular comprehensiveness of Hinduism, the Theosophical movement does not appear to be regarded as an alien cult, though, to our minds, it appears as widely separate from Hinduism as practised as it is from Christianity.

If we say that the chief work of missionaries must be educational, it must be understood that by education, reading and writing are not alone meant. Taken by themselves those arts would be small objects of missionary effort. We mean by education, the training of mind towards the Christian ideals of honesty, fair dealing, and truthfulness, and the abolition of all customs which are incompatible with the teaching of Christ. The Government abolished suttee, and the marriage of widows is legal. But how few widows will public opinion allow to marry? There is no power in law that can forbid child marriages, but there could be most potent influence used in modifying its abuses without interfering with racial doctrines; respect for life should be shown to be compatible with the death of such sorely afflicted creatures as an abuse of a good teaching will not allow a Hindu at present to put out of their misery; obscene and extravagant festivities, and temple abuses—those are but a few of the many customs which are alien to Christianity, which can scarcely be touched by law without great danger to the whole fabric of an ancient civilisation, but which may, in time, yield to the gentler doctrines of Christianity. The problems of the East are very great; our duties as the governing class are manifold. The success of our missions is in many respects highly gratifying, but over all we must remember that East is East and West is West, and therefore once more I venture to say to all who travel in the cause of Christianity in the Far East, "Oh be pitiful, be courteous!"

APPENDICES

I. ITINERARY

1906.

Nov. 6.	Left Glasgow.
7.	Left London.
9.	Left Marseilles on P. and O. *Macedonia.*
23.	Arrived Bombay : Hotel Taj Mahal.
26-28.	Delautabad : Temples of Ellora ; Roza.
29-30.	Bombay : Hotel Taj Mahal.
Dec. 1.	Ahmedabad.
2-6.	Mount Abu, Dilwarra, etc. : Rajputana Hotel.
7.	Ajmere.
8-11.	Udaipur.
12-13.	Chitorgarh and Chitor : Dak Bungalow.
14-17.	Indore : Guests of Rev. Mr. Wilson.
18-20.	Jaipur : Hotel Kaiser-i-Hind.
21-24.	Agra : Hotel Métropole.
25-27.	Delhi : Maidens Hotel.
28.	Amritsar : Cambridge Hotel.
29-30.	Rawal-Pindi : Guests of Rev. R. S. M. Roche.
31.	Arrived at Government House, Lahore : Guests of H.H. Sir Chas. Rivaz.

1907.

Jan. 3.	Left Lahore.
4.	Arrived at Lucknow : Wutzler's Royal Hotel.

1907.	
Jan. 5.	Cawnpore (day excursion).
7.	Left Lucknow: arrived at Benares: Clarke's Hotel.
7-9.	Benares.
10-13.	Calcutta: Guests of Mr. H. C. Begg.
14-15.	Darjeeling: Woodlands Hotel.
16.	Pashok, on way to Kalimpong: Guests of Mr. Lister.
17-18.	Kalimpong: Guests of Rev. Dr. Graham.
19.	Sovoke: Silliguri.
20.	Arrived at Dhubri-ghat, on river Brahmaputra.
20-21.	On river.
21.	Arrived at Gauhati, Assam.
22 to Feb. 4.	Titabur Tea Estate: Guests of Mr. R. G. Black.
4.	Left Titabur.
5.	Cachar Valley.
6.	On river.
7-9.	Calcutta: Guests of Mr. H. C. Begg.
10.	Left Calcutta on B.I. *Taroba*.
12-14.	Rangoon: Royal Hotel.
15-16.	Mandalay: Salween House Hotel.
17-25.	On Irrawaddy flotilla steamers to Bhamo and back.
18.	Kyouckmyoung.
19.	Tagoung.
20.	Tigyang.
21.	Katha.
22.	Arrived at Bhamo.
23.	Left Bhamo.
25.	Arrived at Mandalay.
26-28.	Rangoon: Royal Hotel.
28.	Left Rangoon on B.I. *Bharata*.
March 4.	Penang.
8-9.	Singapore: Raffles' Hotel.
7.	Visit to Johore.

1907.	
March 10.	Left Singapore on German Lloyd *Ziethen*.
15-23.	Hong Kong : Hong Kong Hotel.
18.	Canton.
20-21.	Macao : Macao Hotel.
23.	Left Hong Kong on Japanese *America Maru*.
26.	Shanghai.
28.	Nagasaki.
29.	Arrived at Kobe.
30 to April 8.	Kyoto : Miyako Hotel.
2.	Lake Biwa.
3.	Rapids of Katsura-gawa.
5.	Nara.
8-9.	Nagoya : Nagoya Hotel.
9-12.	Tokyo : Imperial Hotel.
12.	Arrived at Nikko : Kanaya Hotel.
13.	Excursion to Lake Chuzenji.
15.	Left Nikko.
15-17.	Ikao : Lake Haruna, etc. : Ikao Hotel.
17-18.	Myogi : Hotel Hisihi-ya.
18.	Isobe to Tokyo : Imperial Hotel.
19-21.	Miyanoshima : Fugi-ya Hotel.
21.	Lake Hakone : Ten Province Pass, etc., to Atami.
22-23.	Atami to Enoshima, etc. : Kin-ki-eo Hotel.
23-27.	Yokohama.
24.	Tokyo.
26.	Tokyo : Imperial Cherry-Gazing Garden-Party.
28.	Left Japan on *Mongolia*.
May 2.	Double-Day : the second is Antipodes Day.
7-8.	Honolulu : Moana Hotel.
15-17.	San Francisco : Palace Hotel.
17-21.	Del Monte : Monterey, etc. : Hotel Del Monte.
22.	San Francisco : Palace Hotel.
22-27.	Yosemite Valley : Sentinel Hotel : Wawona Hotel.

1907.	
May 28.	San Francisco: left San Francisco.
29-31.	Train delayed at Hornbrook: bridge burned.
31.	Portland, Oregon, and Seattle: Stander Hotel.
June 1.	Left Seattle.
2-4.	Banff: Rocky Mountains: Banff Springs Hotel.
5-7.	Winnipeg: Royal Alexandra Hotel.
9.	Train delayed at Scotia Junction: train coming from east had been upset on track.
9-10.	Toronto: King Edward Hotel.
11-12.	Niagara: Clifton Hotel.
12-13.	Toronto: King Edward Hotel.
14-16.	Quebec: Chateau Frontenac.
16-17.	Montreal: Windsor Hotel.
17-18.	Left Montreal for Plattsburg: steamer *Vernon* down Lake Champlain: Ticonderoga: Lake George and Albany: Hotel Ten Eyck.
19.	Voyage down Hudson to New York.
19-26.	New York: Waldorf-Astoria Hotel.
26.	Left New York on Hamburg-Amerika *Deutschland*.
July 3.	Arrived at Plymouth.
10.	Home.

II. MALAY THEATRE (PAGE 53).

(PAGE 53)

The following was the programme of the Malay Theatre at Singapore two days after our visit:

WAYANG KASSIM.

TO-NIGHT!!

Friday, 8*th March* 1907.

DON'T FORGET! DON'T FORGET!!

A Special Performance

NOW COME NOW

LOSE NO TIME

THE

INDRA-ZANIBAR ROYAL THEATRICAL CO.

OF SINGAPORE.

AT THE ALEXANDRA THEATRE HALL,

NORTH BRIDGE ROAD.

WELL PRODUCE THE SPLENDID PLAY

BAHMAN KHALEK.

THE TWINS

NO SHOW ON SUNDAY NIGHT.

A king has no children and makes an oath that he will give his first child to the church. A geni appears to him while he is making the oath, and promises that he will have a child, on condition he gives it to him. He agrees, and the geni gives him a flower, telling him to dilute it in water and give it to his wife.

He does so and his wife gives birth to twins. They are named Bahman and Khalek, but Bahman the eldest is born mad.

He sends Bahman to the genii in charge of his men, but the Geni does not want him as he is mad, so he sends word to the king ordering him to send the other boy or he will destroy his property.

Fearing the Genii, the king orders Khalek to go to him, and leaving his father he goes away.

A king of bird's daughter is in a wood and a tiger springs out and is about to attack her, when Khalek appears on the scene, killing the tiger rescues her. To show her gratitude, she takes him home.

When her father and mother come to meet her, they did not find her seeing the dead tiger, conclude it has eaten her.

When they go home, they see Khalek and thinking he has killed the girl they are about to slay him when she appears and informs them of his brave deed. They reward him by making her his wife, and he shortly after leaves them to contenue his search of the geni the bird king gives him his wings saying it will help him on his journey.

On his way he meets two fairies who fall in love with him, but as he is troubled about the geni he tell them so and giving them his ring he leaves them.

He now meets the geni and giving himself to him, he adopts him as his son, he gives Khalek a hair of his head telling him to use this when he is in trouble and he will appear they then part.

The king sends for a physician to cure Bahman of his rusaiut and while they are examining him he decamps.

He meets two fairies who are betrothed to two genii and they have some fun with the mad prince, while this is going on, there intended husband the genii appear, and bring angry with the prince take him before their king.

The king orders them to take him to a wood and kill him. While they are about to do so, Khalek his younger brother passes that way and stops them telling them he is his brother. They refuse to listen to him and he summons the geni whose hair he has together they thrash the two genii the geni now cures Bahman and taking the fairies with them, they all return home to the king.

ADMISSION PRICES.

Reserved - - - -	$2.00	Second Class - - -	50 cts.
First Class - - -	,, 1.00	Third ,, - - -	25 ,,

LADIES, 1st. Class 50 cts. 2nd. Class 30 cts.

Overture 8 p.m. — Curtain 9 p.m. — Carriages 12 p.m.

No show on Sunday night. S. KASSIM,—*Sole Proprietor.*

Alwee Brothers, Printers, Singapore.

An advertisement in a Penang newspaper ran as follows:

To-night! To-night!
Dedicated in loving memory of our beloved
Wm. Shakespeare.
The Opera Indra Permato Company of Selangor will stage
the Sensational Tragedy Prince Hamlet,
By the best actors and actresses procurable in Java.
Our clowns are without rivals!
This is actually the best representation of a European
Opera by a Native Company.

CHOW CHONG, Proprietor.

III. HOW WONDER MINING CAMP, NEVADA, SOUGHT A MINISTER.

The following is an excerpt from the *San Francisco Chronicle* of Saturday, May 18, 1907:

MINING CAMP SEEKS PREACHER.

WONDER CITIZENS WANT MINISTER OF ANY CREED EXCEPT BAPTIST.

Special Dispatch to the "Chronicle."

Reno (Nev.), May 17.—Wonder, the promising mining camp in Churchill county, wants a preacher, and wants one bad. In fact, the citizens of that camp have sent James E. Pelton to Reno to endeavor to secure a minister of the gospel to take up his abode at Wonder. They are not particular about the creed, as long as he can say a few prayers, sing a song or two and preach a funeral sermon, except that a Baptist is disqualified from the conditions of the camp. Not that the miners of Wonder have any particular objection to a Baptist minister, but they doubt if a preacher of that denomination could secure any converts, and if he did he could not baptise them according to the rules of his church when an ordinary bath costs $21 a head, owing to the scarcity of water.

In speaking of his mission yesterday Pelton said: "It is just this way. A few days ago one of the boys died and we had no minister to officiate at the funeral. I decided to act if some one would find me a prayer book or Bible, but the camp was searched in vain. I remembered the Lord's Prayer, and this was the only service we were able to give our comrade.

"Right there the boys of the camp decided we must have a preacher, and they have sent me to obtain one. Now I want a sky-pilot who is young and a good fellow, one who can handle a gun if necessary. The boys told me that they wanted a preacher who had forgotten how to swear, but that they wouldn't mind if he drank and smoked a bit and was a real good fellow.

"Now I have nothing against a Baptist minister, but water for immersion at $5 a barrel would sort o' hinder his good work. Any kind of a minister but a Baptist will do. We will pay his fare to Wonder, build him a church and pay him a good salary. He couldn't ask for more for a starter, could he?"

The same journal, a few days afterwards, announced that Wonder had secured its desired minister.

GLASGOW: PRINTED AT THE UNIVERSITY PRESS BY ROBERT MACLEHOSE AND CO. LTD.